The Complete Guitar Player Songbook
Omnibus Edition

by Russ Shipton

Project editors: Jerry Willard and David Bradley

This book Copyright © 2004 by Amsco Publications,
A Division of Music Sales Corporation, New York

Order No. AM 978439
International Standard Book Number: 0.8256.2828.8

Exclusive Distributors:
Music Sales Corporation
257 Park Avenue South, New York, NY 10010 USA
Music Sales Limited
8/9 Frith Street, London W1D 3JB England
Music Sales Pty. Limited
120 Rothschild Street, Rosebery, Sydney, NSW 2018, Australia

Printed in the United States of America by
Vicks Lithograph and Printing Corporation

Amsco Publications
A Part of **The Music Sales Group**
New York/London/Paris/Sydney/Copenhagen/Berlin/Tokyo/Madrid

Contents—Book One

6 Amazing Grace
8 All I Really Want to Do
29 Bad Moon Rising
20 Cecilia
10 Cold, Cold Heart
12 El Condor Pasa
30 Everybody's Talkin'
14 Feelin' Alright
48 For Emily, Whenever I May Find Her
22 Forever Young
66 Greensleeves
73 A Horse with No Name
43 I Am a Man of Constant Sorrow
32 I'll Be Your Baby Tonight
62 Johnny Has Gone for a Soldier
16 Knockin' on Heaven's Door
45 Learning to Fly
50 Let It Rain
26 Like a Rolling Stone
52 Lucky Man
60 Mother and Child Reunion
7 Oh, Bury Me Not on the Lone Prairie
18 Quinn the Eskimo
54 Scarborough Fair
44 Sometimes I Feel Like a Motherless Child
63 The Sound of Silence
34 This Land Is Your Land
56 The Tide Is High
58 The Times They Are A-Changin'
68 Turn! Turn! Turn!
70 Two Tickets to Paradise
38 Visions of Johanna
42 Who'll Stop the Rain
36 Yellow Rose of Texas
24 You Ain't Goin' Nowhere

Contents—Book Two

115 All along the Watchtower
80 Be Thankful for What You've Got
134 Behind Blue Eyes
94 Both Sides Now
108 The Boxer
112 Can You Feel the Love Tonight
103 Candle in the Wind
118 Chelsea Morning
82 Father and Son
156 Fly Me to the Moon
153 Hard Headed Woman
120 Homeward Bound
114 House of the Rising Sun
78 I Am a Rock
132 I Want You
85 If Not for You
96 I'll Be
106 It Ain't Me Babe
122 La Bamba
140 Leaving on a Jet Plane
128 Lemon Tree
88 Maggie May
160 Mrs. Robinson
102 Morning Has Broken
99 Oh, Pretty Woman
142 Puff the Magic Dragon
144 Rainy Day Women #12 & 35
130 Superstar
137 Tainted Love
150 Take Me Home, Country Roads
146 Teach Your Children
125 That's How Strong My Love Is
157 Tonight I'll Be Staying Here with You
148 Wild World
90 Wonderful Tonight
92 Woodstock

Contents—Book Three

206 America
194 Annie's Song
222 April Come She Will
200 Baby Hold On
196 The Best of My Love
170 Bridge Over Troubled Water
224 Endless Love
231 Fifty Ways to Leave Your Lover
176 Goodbye Yellow Brick Road
188 Helplessly Hoping
191 I Feel the Earth Move
219 I Remember You
228 Jesus Is Just Alright
166 Killing Me Softly
203 Kodachrome™
234 Lay, Lady, Lay
168 Leader of the Band
210 Let's Groove
226 Lovin' You
178 Make You Feel My Love
173 Perfect World
238 Rainy Days and Mondays
213 Rocket Man
220 Send in the Clowns
180 Simple Twist of Fate
182 Sorry Seems to Be the Hardest Word
216 Still Crazy after All These Years
198 What a Difference a Day Makes
184 What a Wonderful World
186 You Are So Beautiful

The Complete Guitar Player Songbook

Book 1

by Russ Shipton

6   Amazing Grace
7   Oh, Bury Me Not on the Lone Prairie
8   All I Really Want to Do
10   Cold, Cold Heart
12   El Condor Pasa
14   Feelin' Alright +
16   Knockin' on Heaven's Door +
18   Quinn the Eskimo
20   Cecilia +
22   Forever Young
24   You Ain't Goin' Nowhere
26   Like a Rolling Stone +
29   Bad Moon Rising +
30   Everybody's Talkin'
32   I'll Be Your Baby Tonight
34   This Land Is Your Land
36   Yellow Rose of Texas
38   Visions of Johanna

42   Who'll Stop the Rain
43   I Am a Man of Constant Sorrow
44   Sometimes I Feel Like a Motherless Child
45   Learning to Fly
48   For Emily, Whenever I May Find Her
50   Let It Rain
52   Lucky Man
54   Scarborough Fair
56   The Tide Is High
58   The Times They Are A-Changin'
60   Mother and Child Reunion
62   Johnny Has Gone for a Soldier
63   The Sound of Silence
66   Greensleeves
68   Turn! Turn! Turn!
70   Two Tickets to Paradise
73   A Horse with No Name +

Amsco Publications
A Part of **The Music Sales Group**
New York/London/Paris/Sydney/Copenhagen/Berlin/Tokyo/Madrid

Amazing Grace John Newton

Bass-strum style

2. 'Twas grace that taught my heart to fear,
   And grace my fears relieved;
   How precious did that grace appear
   The hour I first believed.

3. Through many dangers, toils, and snares
   I have already come;
   'Tis grace hath brought me safe thus far,
   And grace will lead me home.

6

Oh, Bury Me Not on the Lone Prairie — Traditional

Bass-strum style T ↓ ↑ T ↓ ↑
1 2 & 3 4 &

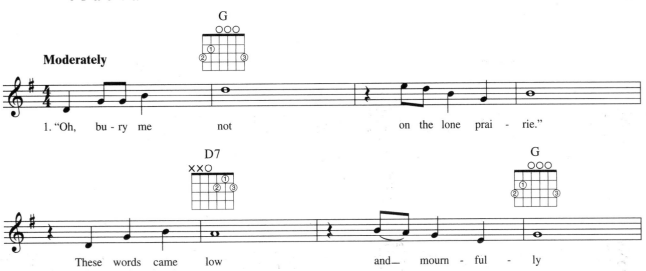

Moderately

1. "Oh, bu - ry me not   on the lone prai - rie."

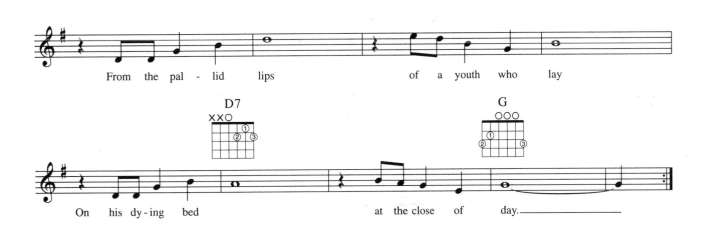

These words came low   and— mourn - ful - ly

From the pal - lid lips   of a youth who lay

On his dy - ing bed   at the close of day.

2. He moaned in pain while over his head
   The shadows of death grew thick like lead;
   He thought of his home and family that night
   As the cowboys gathered to watch him die.

3. "Oh, bury me not on the lone prairie
   Where the wild coyotes howl over me,
   In a narrow grave, just six by three.
   Oh, bury me not on the lone prairie.

4. "In dreams I've listened to the well-known words
   Of the wild prairie winds and the songs of birds;
   I think of the table where my mama put flowers
   And the scenes I loved in those long lost hours.

5. "It matters not I've often been told,
   Where the body lies when the heart grows cold;
   Oh, grant, oh grant this wish to me
   And bury me not on the lone prairie.

6. "I've always wished to be laid when I died
   In a little churchyard on the green hillside;
   By my mama's grave please let mine be,
   And bury me not on the lone prairie."

7. "Oh, bury me not... " And his voice stopped there.
   But we took no heed of his dyin' prayer;
   In a narrow grave, just six by three
   We buried him there, on the lone prairie.

All I Really Want to Do   Bob Dylan

Bass-strum style T ↓ ↑ ↓
                  1 2 & 3

Moderately bright

1. I ain't look-in' to com-pete with you, Beat or
   I ain't look-in' to___ fight with you, Fright-en

cheat or mis-treat you. Sim-pli-fy you,
you or tight-en you. Drag you down or

clas-si-fy you, De-ny, de-fy or cru-ci-
drain you down,___ Chain you down or bring you

fy you All I___ real-ly___ want to
down.___

do___ is, ba-by, be friends with

| 1.- 5. | 6. |

you.___   2. No and

3.   I ain't lookin' to block you up,
Shock or knock or lock you up,
Analyze you, categorize you,
Finalize you or advertise you.
All I really want to do
Is, baby, be friends with you.

4.   I don't want to straight-face you,
Race or chase you, track or trace you,
Or disgrace you or displace you,
Or define you or confine you.
All I really want to do
Is, baby, be friends with you.

5.   I don't want to meet your kin,
Make you spin or do you in,
Or select you or dissect you,
Or inspect you or reject you.
All I really want to do
Is, baby, make friends with you.

6.   I don't want to fake you out,
Take or shake or forsake you out,
I ain't lookin' for you to feel like me,
See like me or be like me.
All I really want to do
Is, baby, be friends with you.

Cold Cold Heart   Hank Williams

Bass-strum style T ↓ T ↓
                  1 2 3 4

Moderately

1. I tried so hard my dear, to show that you're my ev - 'ry

dream. Yet you're a - fraid each thing I do is just some e - vil

scheme. A mem - 'ry from your lone - some past keeps us so far a -

part. Why can't I free your doubt - ful mind and melt your cold, cold

heart? 2. An - oth - er love be - fore my time made your heart sad and

blue. And so my heart is pay - ing now for things I did - n't

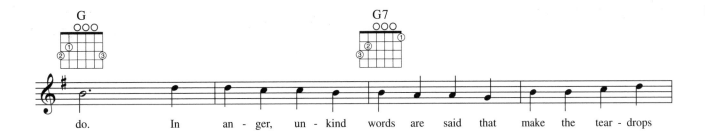

do. In an - ger, un - kind words are said that make the tear - drops

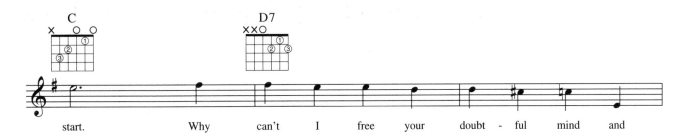

start. Why can't I free your doubt - ful mind and

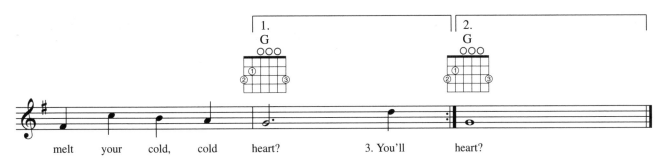

melt your cold, cold heart? 3. You'll heart?

3. You'll never know how much it hurts to see you sit and cry.
You know you need and want my love yet you're afraid to try.
Why do you run and hide from life, To try it just ain't smart.
Why can't I free your doubtful mind and melt your cold cold heart?

4. There was a time when I believed that you belonged to me.
But now I know your heart is shackled to a memory.
The more I learn to care for you, the more we drift apart.
Why can't I free your doubtful mind and melt your cold cold heart?

El Condor Pasa (If I Could)

English Lyrics by Paul Simon
Musical arrangement by Jorge Milchbe
and Daniel Robles

Strumming style ↓ ↑ ↓ ↑ ↓ ↑ ↓ ↑
1 & 2 & 3 & 4 &

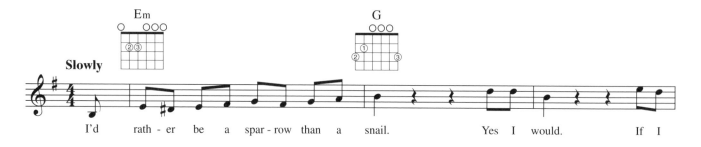

Slowly

I'd rath - er be a spar - row than a snail. Yes I would. If I

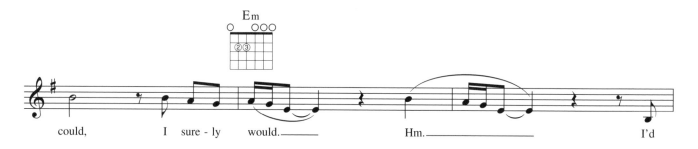

could, I sure - ly would._____ Hm._____ I'd

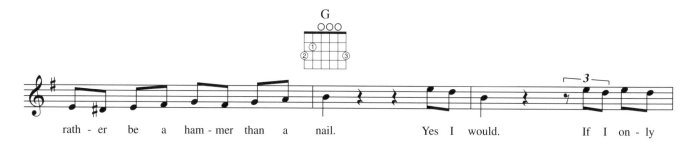

rath - er be a ham - mer than a nail. Yes I would. If I on - ly

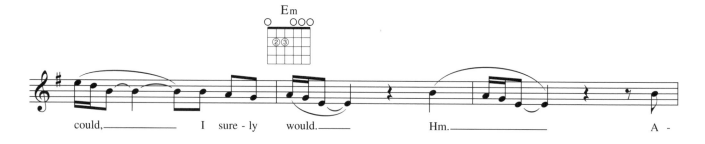

could,_____ I sure - ly would._____ Hm._____ A -

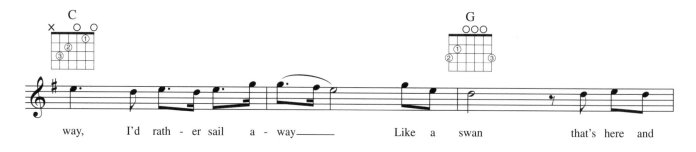

way, I'd rath - er sail a - way_____ Like a swan that's here and

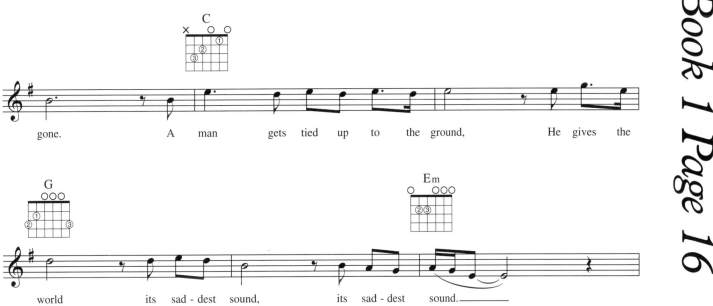

gone.   A man gets tied up to the ground,   He gives the

world   its sad - dest sound,   its sad - dest sound._____

I'd rath - er be a for - est than a

street.   Yes I would.   If I could,_____ I sure - ly

would._____ I'd rath - er feel the earth be - neath my feet.   Yes I

would. If I on - ly could,_____ I sure - ly would._____

Feelin' Alright
Dave Mason

Strumming style ↓ ↓ ↑ ↓ ↑ ↓
          1 2 & 3 & 4

Moderately

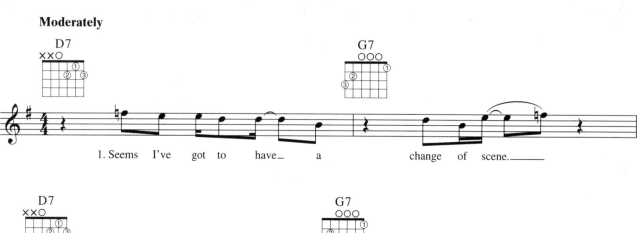

1. Seems I've got to have— a change of scene.___

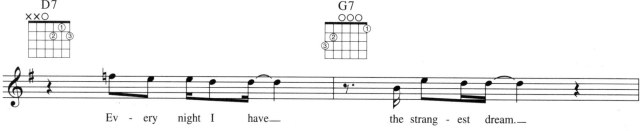

Ev - ery night I have— the strang - est dream.—

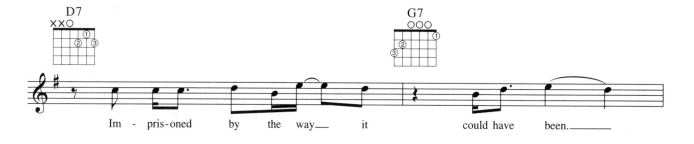

Im - pris-oned by the way— it could have been.___

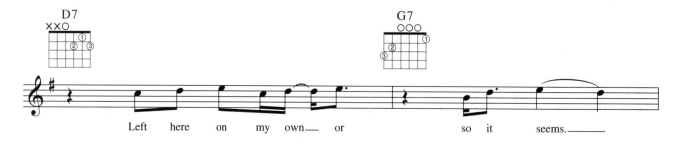

Left here on my own— or so it seems.___

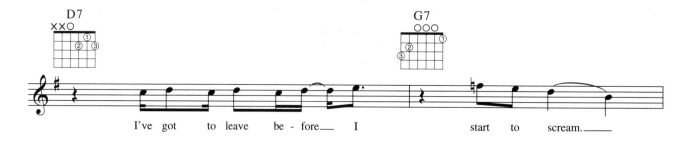

I've got to leave be - fore— I start to scream.___

'Cause some - one locked the door— and— took the key.— Feel - in'

al - right, I'm not feel - in' too good— my - self.

Yes, I'm feel - in' al - right, I'm not feel - in' that good—

1.- 2. 3. *D.S. and fade*

— my - self. Feel - in'

2. Boy you shelter me with warmth and rye.
   And even now I sit and I wonder why
   That when I think of you, I start myself to cry.
   Just can't waste my time, I must get by.
   Gotta stop believin' in all your lies.
   Well there's too much to do before I die.

   Feelin' alright, I'm not feelin' too good myself.
   Feelin' alright, I'm not feelin' too good myself.

3. Ooh, don't you get too lost, in all I say.
   In a better time, you know I really found that way.
   But that was then, and now you know it's today.
   I can't get set for it, guess I'm here to stay,
   Till someone comes along and takes my place,
   With a different name, and a different face.

   Feelin' alright, I'm not feelin' too good myself.
   Feelin' alright, I'm not feelin' too good myself.

Knockin' on Heaven's Door   Bob Dylan

Bass-strum style T ↓ T ↑ ↓
1 2 3 & 4

Slowly

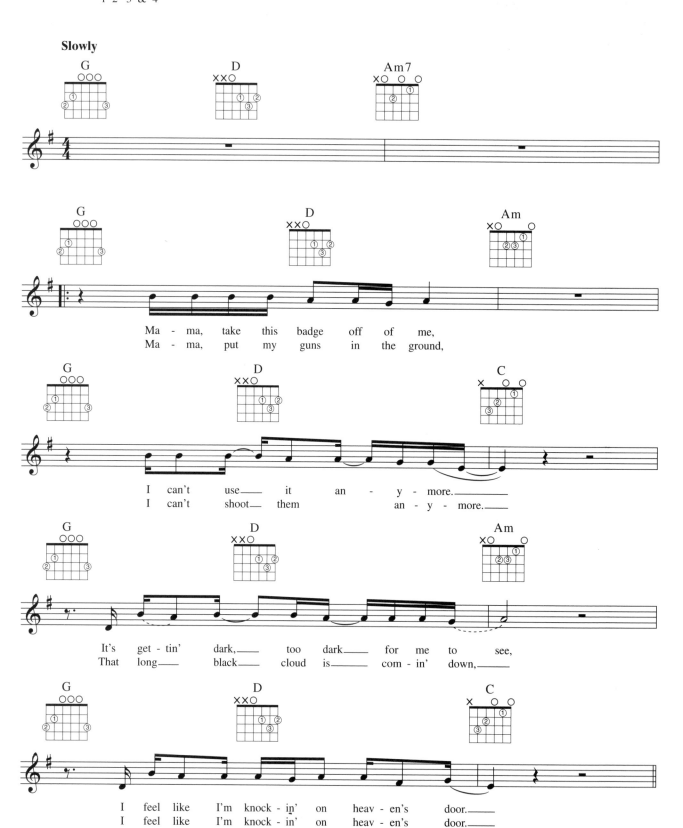

Ma - ma, take this badge off of me,
Ma - ma, put my guns in the ground,

I can't use — it an - y - more. _____
I can't shoot them an - y - more. _____

It's get - tin' dark, ____ too dark ____ for me to see,
That long ____ black ____ cloud is ____ com - in' down, ____

I feel like I'm knock - in' on heav - en's door. ____
I feel like I'm knock - in' on heav - en's door. ____

16

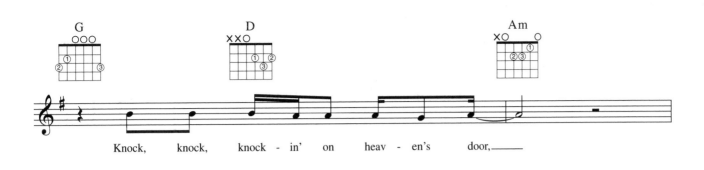

Knock, knock, knock - in' on heav - en's door, _____

Knock, knock, knock - in' on heav - en's door, _____

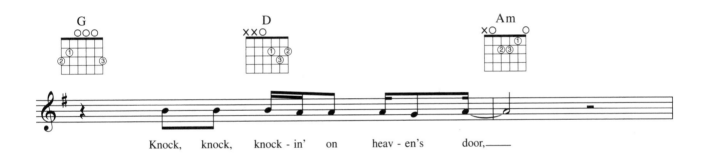

Knock, knock, knock - in' on heav - en's door, _____

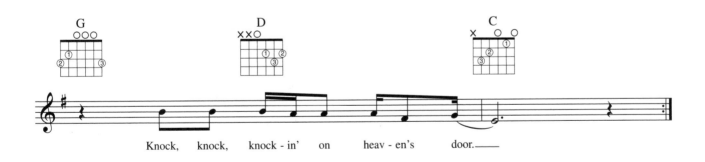

Knock, knock, knock - in' on heav - en's door. _____

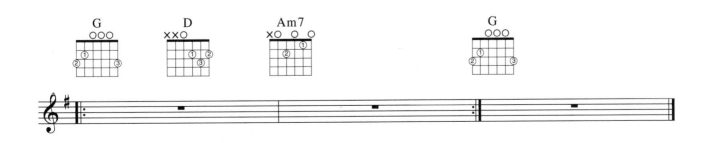

Quinn the Eskimo (The Mighty Quinn)

Bob Dylan

Strumming style ↓ ↓ ↓ ↓
          1 2 3 4

Moderately

1. Ev - 'ry - bod - y's build - ing the big ships and the boats, Some are build - ing mon - u - ments,— oth - ers jot - ting down notes, Ev - 'ry - bod - y's in de - spair, ev - 'ry girl and boy But when Quinn, the Es - ki - mo, gets here, ev - 'ry - bod - y's gon - na jump for joy.—

Chorus

Come all with - out, Come all with - in, You'll

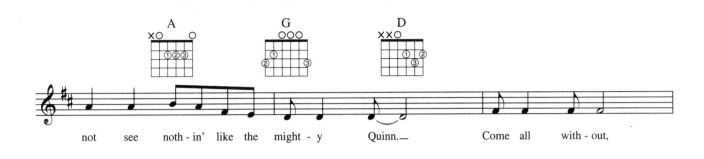

not see noth - in' like the might - y Quinn.— Come all with - out,

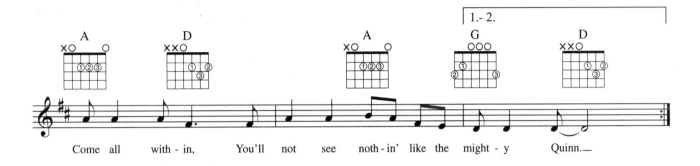

Come all with - in, You'll not see noth - in' like the might - y Quinn.—

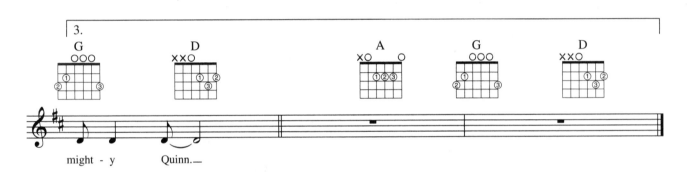

might - y Quinn.—

2. I like to do just like the rest, I like my sugar sweet,
But guarding fumes and making haste,
It ain't my cup of meat,
Everybody's 'neath the trees,
Feeding pigeons on a limb,
But when Quinn, the Eskimo, gets here,
All the pigeons gonna run to him.
Chorus

3. A cat's meow and a cow's moo, I can recite 'em all,
Just tell me where it hurts yuh, honey,
And I'll tell you who to call.
Nobody can get no sleep,
There's someone on everyone's toes,
But when Quinn, the Eskimo, gets here,
Everybody's gonna wanna doze.
Chorus

Cecilia   Paul Simon

Strumming style ↓ ↑ ↓ ↑ ↓ ↑ ↓ ↑
  1 & 2 & 3 & 4 &

Moderately

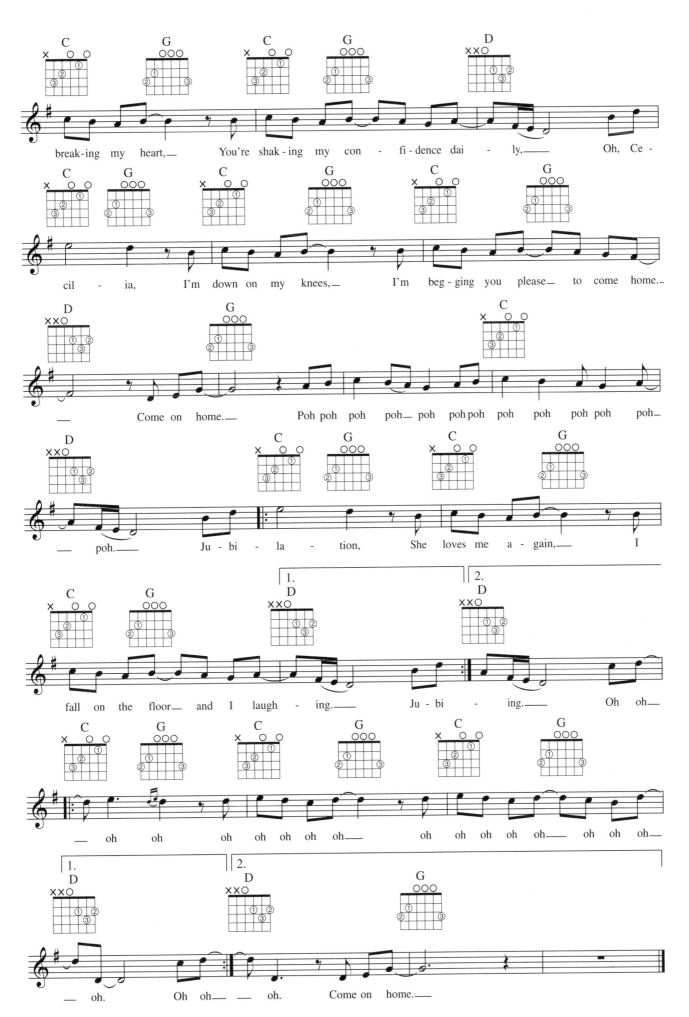

Forever Young   Bob Dylan

Strumming style ↓ ↓ ↓ ↓
        1 2 3 4

Moderately slow

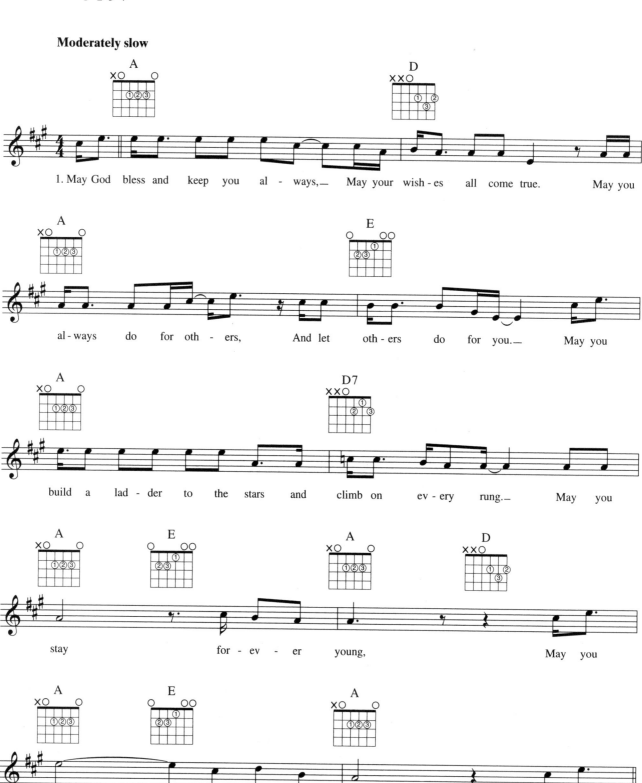

1. May God bless and keep you al - ways,— May your wish - es all come true.   May you

al - ways do for oth - ers,   And let oth - ers do for you.—   May you

build a lad - der to the stars and climb on ev - ery rung.—   May you

stay   for - ev - er young,   May you

stay—   for - ev - er young.   2. May you

You Ain't Goin' Nowhere
Bob Dylan

Strumming style ↓ ↓ ↑ ↓ ↑ ↓
1 2 & 3 & 4

Moderately

1. Clouds so swift,— Rain won't lift,— Gate won't close,—

Rail - ings froze.— Get your mind— off win - ter time,—

You ain't go - in' no - where.— Whoo - ee!— Ride me high,— To -

mor - row's the day My bride's gon - na come. Oh, oh,— Are

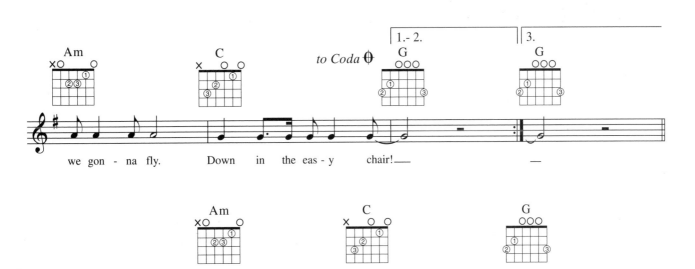

Am — we gon - na fly. — C — Down in the eas - y chair!— — G — G —

1.- 2. **3.**

Am — 4. Gen - ghis Khan,— he could not keep— C — All his kings— sup - plied with sleep.—

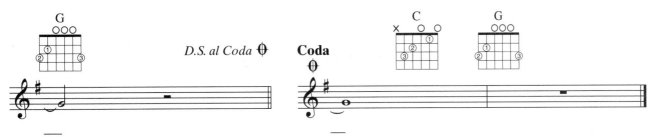

Am — We'll climb that hill,— No mat - ter how steep,— C — When we get up to it.—

G — *D.S. al Coda* — **Coda** — C — G —

2. I don't care
   How many letters they sent
   Morning came and morning went
   Pick up your money
   And pack up your tent
   You ain't goin' nowhere
   Chorus

3. Buy me a flute
   And a gun that shoots
   Tailgates and substitutes
   Strap yourself
   To the tree with roots
   You ain't goin' nowhere
   Chorus

Like A Rolling Stone   Bob Dylan

Strumming style ↓ ↓ ↑ ↓ ↑ ↓
              1 2 & 3 & 4

Brighty

1. Once up - on a time you dressed so fine You

threw the bums a dime in your prime,

Did - n't you People'd call, say,

"Be - ware doll, you're bound to fall" You thought they were all

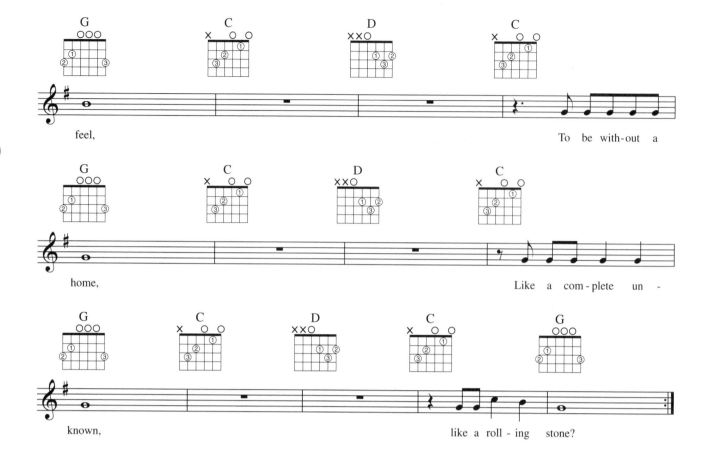

feel,   To be with-out a

home,   Like a com-plete un -

known,   like a roll - ing stone?

2. You've gone to the finest school all right, Miss Lonely
But you know you only used to get juiced in it
And nobody has ever taught you how to live on the street
And now you find out you're gonna have to get used to it
You said you'd never compromise
With the mystery tramp, but now you realize
He's not selling any alibis
As you stare into the vacuum of his eyes
And ask him do you want to make a deal?
Chorus

3. You never turned around to see the frowns on the jugglers and the clowns
When they all come down and did tricks for you
You never understood that it ain't no good
You shouldn't let other people get your kicks for you
You used to ride on the chrome horse with your diplomat
Who carried on his shoulder a Siamese cat
Ain't it hard when you discover that
He really wasn't where it's at
After he took from you everything he could steal.
Chorus

4. Princess on the steeple and all the pretty people
They're drinkin', thinkin' that they got it made
Exchanging all kinds of precious gifts and things
But you'd better lift your diamond ring, you'd better pawn it babe
You used to be so amused
At Napoleon in rags and the language that he used
Go to him now, he calls you, you can't refuse
When you got nothing, you got nothing to lose
You're invisible now, you got no secrets to conceal.
Chorus

Bad Moon Rising J.C. Fogerty

Strumming style ↓ ↓ ↑ ↓ ↓ ↓ ↓
          1 & (2)a & 3 & 4 &

Moderately

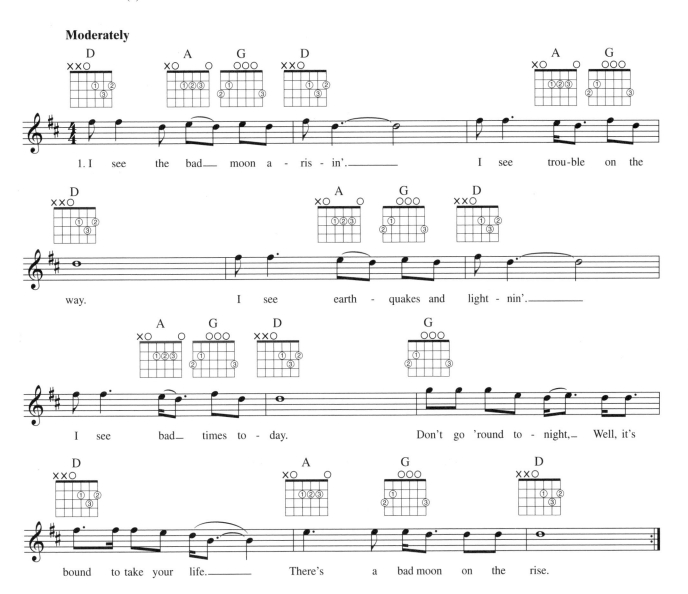

1. I see the bad— moon a - ris - in'._____   I see trou-ble on the

way.   I see earth - quakes and light - nin'._____

I see bad— times to - day.   Don't go 'round to - night,__ Well, it's

bound to take your life._____ There's a bad moon on the rise.

2. I hear hurricanes a-blowing.
   I know the end is coming soon.
   I fear rivers overflowing.
   I hear the voice of rage and ruin.

3. Hope you got your things together.
   Hope you are quite prepared to die.
   Looks like we're in for nasty weather.
   One eye is taken for an eye.

Everybody's Talkin' Fred Neil

Bass-strum style T ↓ ↑ ↓ ↑ ↓ ↑
1 2 & 3 & 4 &

Ev - ery - bod - y's   talk - in' at___ me,   I   don't hear a

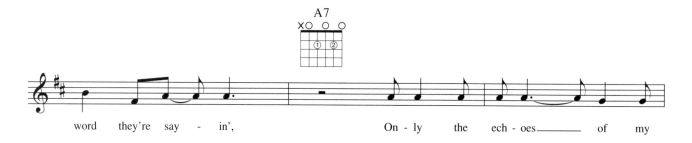

word   they're say - in',   On - ly   the   ech - oes_____ of my

to Coda ⊕

mind._____   Peo - ple stop - pin',   star - in',

I   can't   see   the   fac - es,   On - ly   the

shad - ows___ of their eyes.___   I'm   go - in' where the

I'll Be Your Baby Tonight   Bob Dylan

Strumming style ↓ ↓ ↑ ↓ ↑ ↓
1 2 & 3 & 4

Moderately

Close your eyes,_____ Close the door,_____
light,_____ Shut the shade,_____

— You don't have to wor-ry_____ an-y-more,
— you don't— have_____ to be a-fraid,

— I'll_____ be your_____

_____ ba-by to-night._____

Shut the — Well, that

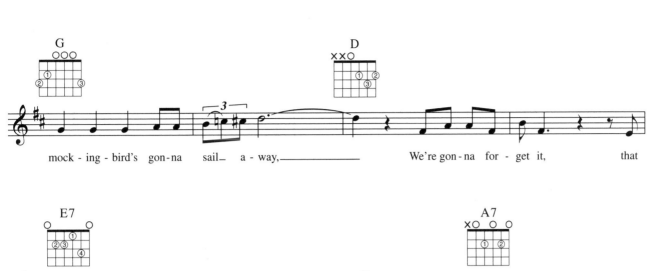

mock - ing - bird's gon - na sail a - way,_____ We're gon - na for - get it, that

big, fat moon_ is gon - na shine like a spoon,_ But, we're gon - na let it,

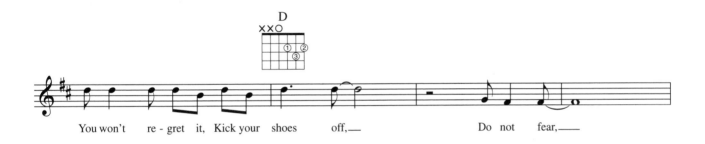

You won't re - gret it, Kick your shoes off,_ Do not fear,_

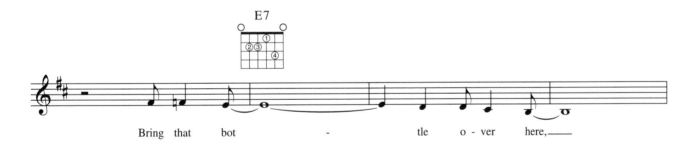

Bring that bot - tle o - ver here,_

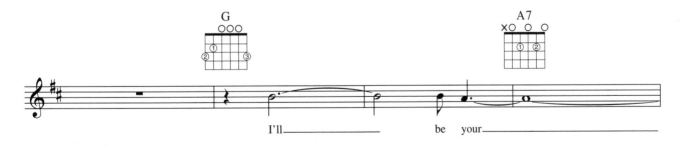

I'll_____ be your_____

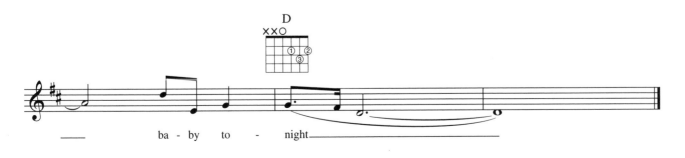

_____ ba - by to - night_____

This Land Is Your Land   Woody Guthrie

Bass-strum style T ↓ T ↑ ↓
1 2 3 & 4

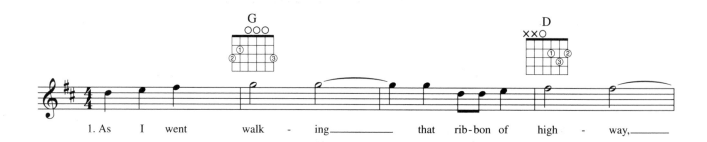

1. As I went walk - ing_____ that rib-bon of high - way,_____

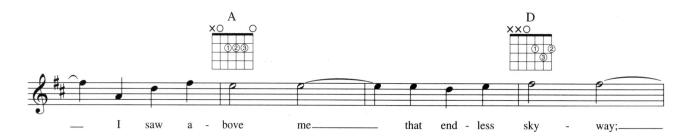

— I saw a - bove me_____ that end - less sky - way;_____

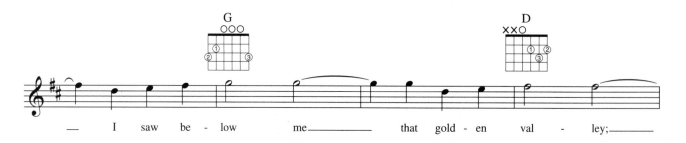

— I saw be - low me_____ that gold - en val - ley;_____

— This land was made for you and me.

Chorus

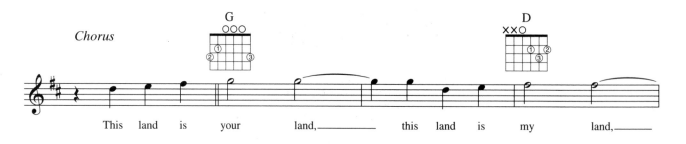

This land is your land,_____ this land is my land,_____

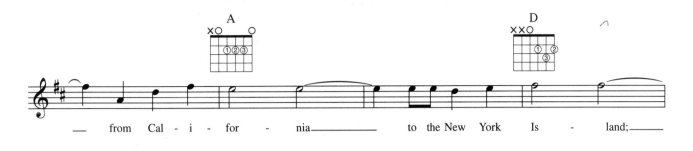

— from Cal - i - for - nia_____ to the New York Is - land;_____

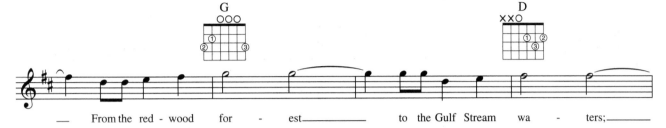

— From the red - wood for - est_____ to the Gulf Stream wa - ters;_____

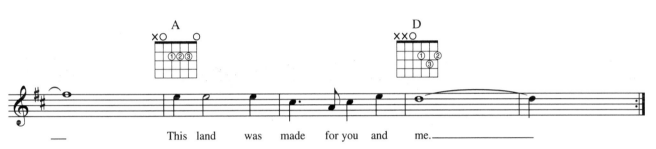

— This land was made for you and me._____

2. I've roamed and rambled, and I've followed my footsteps
   To the sparkling sands of her diamond deserts,
   And all around me a voice was sounding:
   This land was made for you and me.
   Chorus

3. The sun comes shining as I was strolling,
   The wheat fields waving and the dust clouds rolling.
   The fog was lifting a voice come chanting:
   This land was made for you and me.
   Chorus

4. As I was walkin', I saw a sign there,
   And that sign said No Trespassin',
   But on the other side it didn't say nothin'
   Now that side was made for you and me!
   Chorus

5. In the squares of the city, in the shadow of the steeple,
   Near the relief office I see my people.
   And some are grumblin', and some are wonderin'
   If this land's still made for you and me.
   Chorus

6. Nobody living can ever stop me
   As I go walking that freedom highway.
   Nobody living can make me turn back:
   This land was made for you and me.
   Chorus

Yellow Rose of Texas   Traditional

Bass-strum style T ↓ T ↓
1 2 3 4

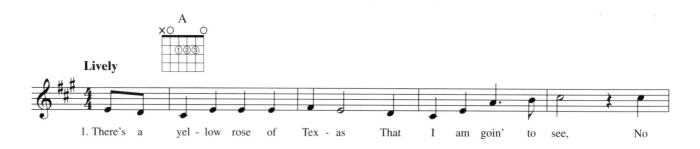

Lively

1. There's a yel - low rose of Tex - as That I am goin' to see, No

oth - er fel - low loves her, No - bod - y, on - ly me. She cried so when I

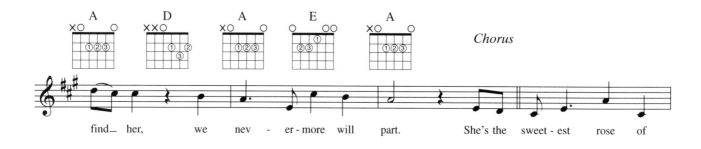

left her, It like to broke my heart And if I ev - er

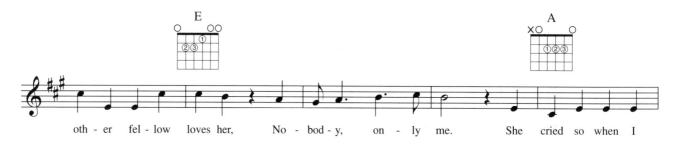

Chorus

find— her, we nev - er - more will part. She's the sweet - est rose of

col - or. This fel - low ev - er knew, Her eyes are bright as

dia - monds— They spar - kle like the dew. You may talk a - bout your

dear - est May, And sing of Ro - sa Lee But the

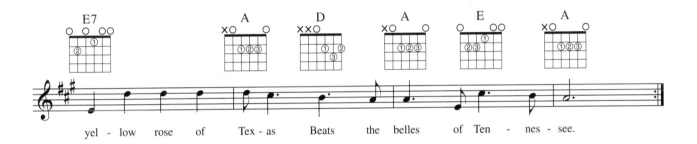

yel - low rose of Tex - as Beats the belles of Ten - nes - see.

2. Where the Rio Grande is flowing
And the starry skies are bright,
She walks along the river
In the quiet summer night,
She thinks if I remember
When we parted long ago,
I promised to come back again
And never leave her so.
Chorus

3. Oh now I'm going to find her
For my hearts is full of woe,
And we'll sing the song together
That we sang so long ago.
We'll play the banjo gaily,
And we'll sing the song of yore,
And the yellow rose of Texas
Shall be mine for ever more.
Chorus

Book 1 Pages 8-11

Visions of Johanna

Bob Dylan

Strumming style ↓ ↓ ↓ ↓
1 2 3 4

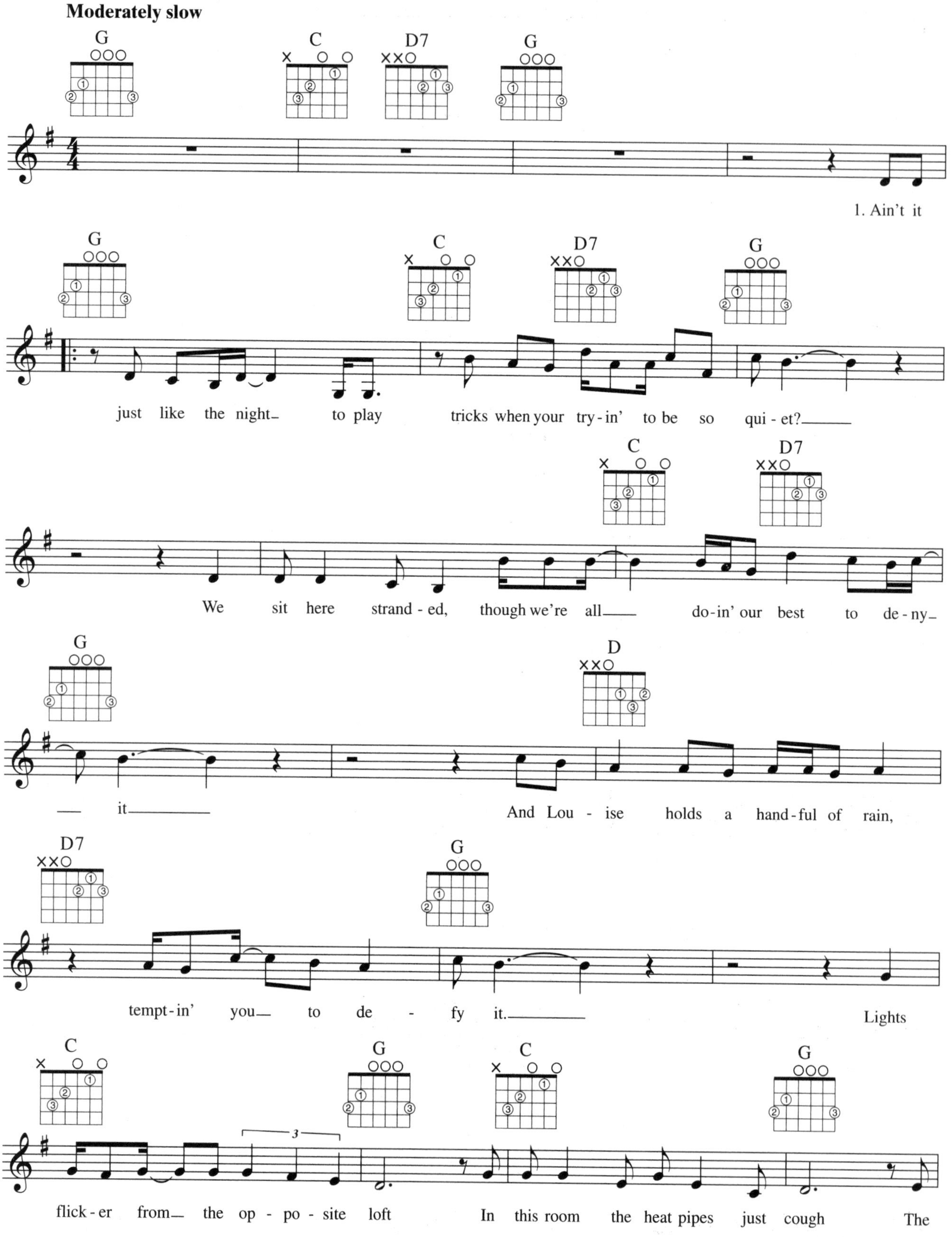
Moderately slow
G C D7 G
1. Ain't it
G C D7 G
just like the night_ to play tricks when your try-in' to be so qui-et?___
C D7
We sit here strand-ed, though we're all___ do-in' our best to de-ny_
G D
__ it_____ And Lou-ise holds a hand-ful of rain,
D7 G
tempt-in' you_ to de-fy it.___ Lights
C G C G
flick-er from_ the op-po-site loft In this room the heat pipes just cough The

for him"   But like Lou - ise___ al - ways says,___ "Ya can't

look   at   much,___ can   ya man?" As she, her - self,   pre - pares   for him___

And   Ma - don - na, she still___ has   not   showed   We   see this

emp - ty   cage___ now   cor - rode   Where her   cape   of   the   stage once   had

flowed   The fid - dler,   he   now   steps   to   the   road   He   writes

ev - 'ry - thing's   been re - turned   which   was   owed   On   the   back___

___ of   the fish truck that   loads___ While my   con - science ex - plodes   The   har -

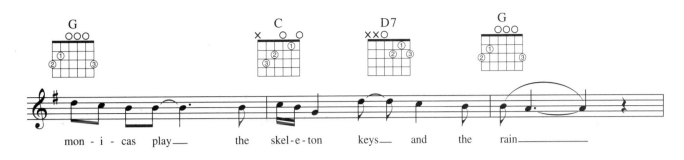

mon - i - cas play— the skel - e - ton keys— and the rain—

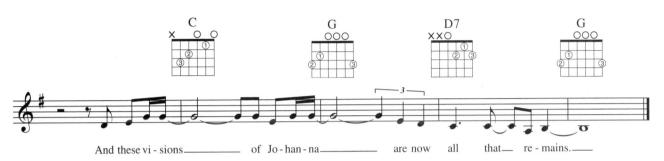

And these vi - sions——— of Jo - han - na——— are now all that— re - mains.——

2. In the empty lot where the ladies play blindman's bluff with the key chain
   And the all-night girls they whisper of escapades out on the "D" train
   We can hear the night watchman click his flashlight
   Ask himself if it's him or them that's really insane
   Louise, she's all right, she's just near
   She's delicate and seems like the mirror
   But she just makes it all too concise and too clear
   That Johanna's not here
   The ghost of 'lectricity howls in the bones of her face
   Where these visions of Johanna have now taken my place

3. Now, little boy lost, he takes himself so seriously
   He brags of his misery, he likes to live dangerously
   And when bringing her name up
   He speaks of a farewell kiss to me
   He's sure got a lotta gall to be so useless and all
   Muttering small talk at the wall while I'm in the hall
   How can I explain?
   Oh, it's so hard to get on
   And these visions of Johanna, they kept me up past the dawn

4. Inside the museums, Infinity goes up on trial
   Voices echo this is what salvation must be like after a while
   But Mona Lisa musta had the highway blues
   You can tell by the way she smiles
   See the primitive wallflower freeze
   When the jelly-faced women all sneeze
   Hear the one with the mustache say, "Jeeze
   I can't find my knees"
   Oh, jewels and binoculars hang from the head of the mule
   But these visions of Johanna, they make it all seem so cruel

Who'll Stop the Rain   J.C. Fogerty

Bass-strum style   T ↑ ↓ ↑ T ↑ ↓ ↑
1 & 2 & 3 & 4 &

Moderately

1. Long as I___ re - mem - ber the rain been com-in' down.

Clouds of mys - tery pour - in' con - fu - sion on the ground.___

Good men through___ the a - ges tryin' to find___ a sun,

And I won - der, still I won - der, Who'll stop the rain?___

2. I went down Virginia
   Seeking shelter from the storm.
   Caught up in the fable
   I watched the tower grow.
   About your plans for new year,
   Wrapped in golden chains,
   And I wonder, still I wonder
   Who'll stop the rain?

3. Heard the singers playing
   How I cheered for more.
   The crowd had rushed together
   Trying to keep warm.
   And still the rain kept falling,
   Falling on my head.
   And I wonder, still I wonder
   Who'll stop the rain?

I Am a Man of Constant Sorrow

Traditional

Bass-strum T ↓ ↓ ↑ ↓
1 2 3 & 4

1. I am a man of con - stant sor - row, I've seen trou - ble all my days. I bid fare - well to old Ken - tuck - y, The place where I was born and raised.

2. For six long years I've been in trouble
No pleasures here on earth I found.
For in this world I'm bound to ramble
I have no friends to help me now.

3. It's fare thee well my old lover
I never expect to see you again.
For I'm bound to ride that northern railroad
Perhaps I'll die upon this train.

4. You can bury me in some deep valley
For many years where I may lay.
Then you may learn to love another
While I am sleeping in my grave.

5. Maybe your friends think I'm just a stranger
My face you'll never see no more.
But there is one promise that is given
I'll meet you on God's golden shore.

Sometimes I Feel Like a Motherless Child

Traditional

Arpeggio style T i m r
1 & 2 &

Slowly

1. Some - times I feel like a moth - er - less child,____
2. Some - times I feel like I'm al - most gone,____

Some - times I feel like a moth - er - less child,____
Some - times I feel like I'm al - most gone,____

Some - times I feel like a moth - er - less child,____ }
Some - times I feel like I'm al - most gone,____ }   A

long ways____ from home,_____   A

long ways____ from home._____

Learning to Fly

Jeff Lynne and Tom Petty

Strumming style ↓ ↑ ↓ ↑ ↑ ↓ ↑
1 & 2 & (3)& 4 &

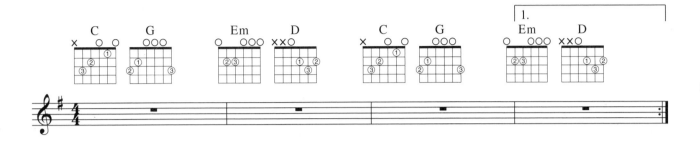

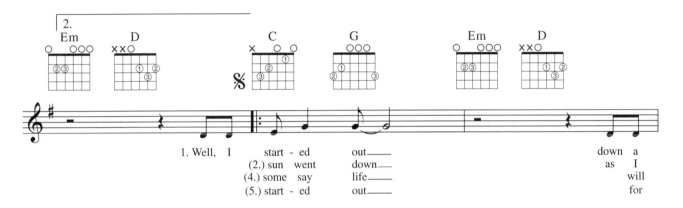

1. Well, I start - ed out____ down a
(2.) sun went down____ as I
(4.) some say life____ will
(5.) start - ed out____ for

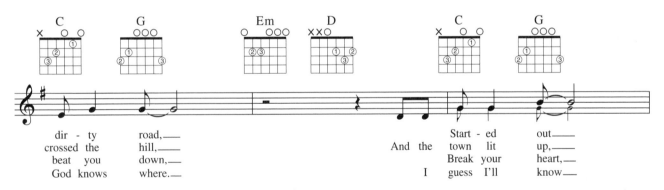

dir - ty road,____ Start - ed out____
crossed the hill,____ And the town lit up,____
beat you down,____ Break your heart,____
God knows where.____ I guess I'll know____

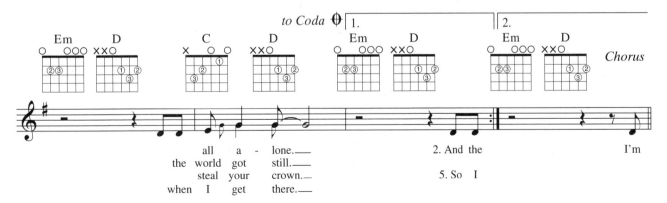

to Coda ⊕

Chorus

all a - lone.____ 2. And the I'm
the world got still.____
steal your crown.____ 5. So I
when I get there.____

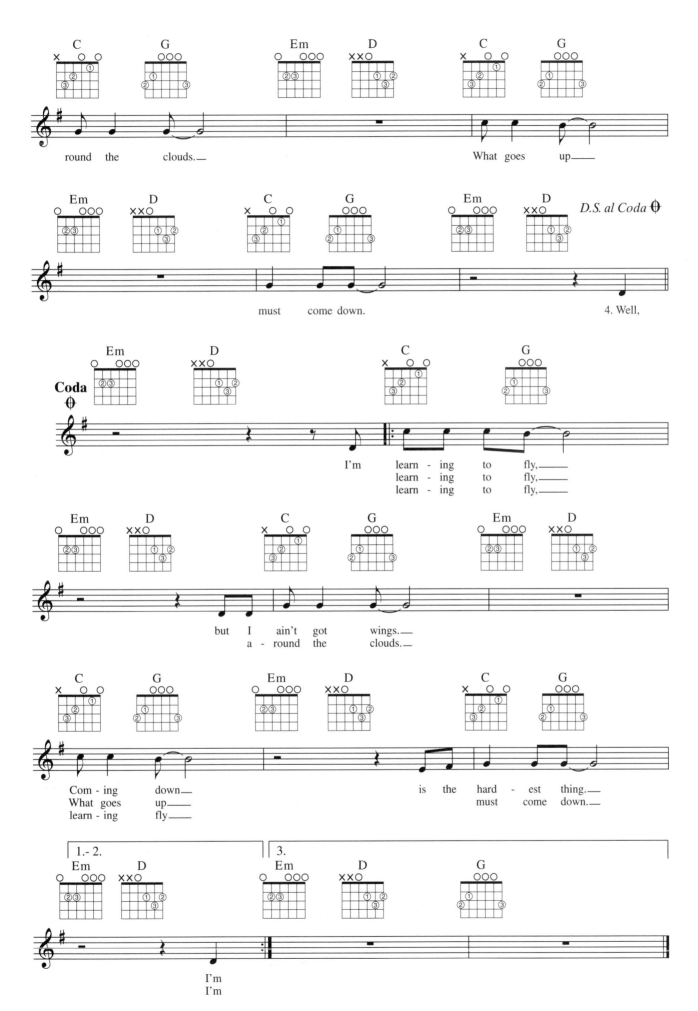

For Emily, Whenever I May Find Her   Paul Simon

Arpeggio T i m i T r m i
1 & 2 & 3 & 4 &

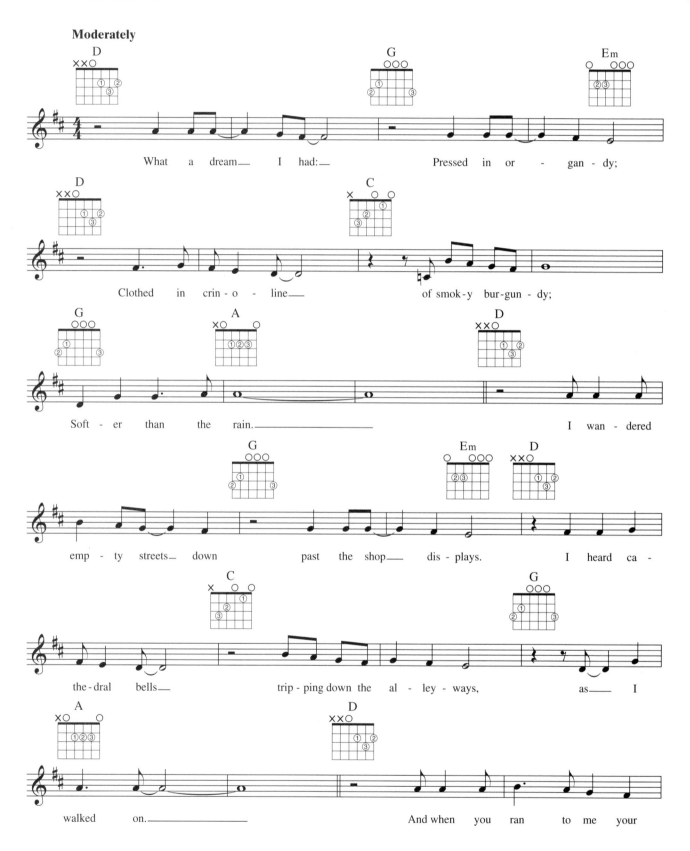

Moderately

What a dream__ I had:__ Pressed in or - gan - dy;

Clothed in crin - o - line__ of smok - y bur - gun - dy;

Soft - er than the rain._____ I wan - dered

emp - ty streets__ down past the shop__ dis - plays. I heard ca -

the - dral bells__ trip - ping down the al - ley - ways, as__ I

walked on._____ And when you ran to me your

Let It Rain

Bonnie Bramlett and Eric Clapton

Strumming style ↓ ↓ ↑   ↑ ↓
1 2 & (3) & 4

Bright rock beat

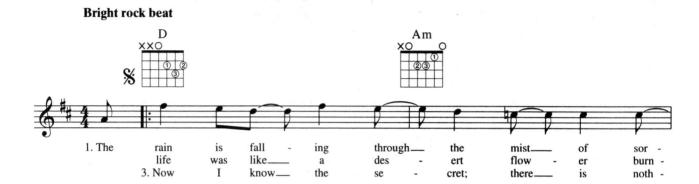

1. The rain is fall - ing through___ the mist___ of sor -
   life was like___ a des - ert flow - er burn -
3. Now I know___ the se - cret; there___ is noth -

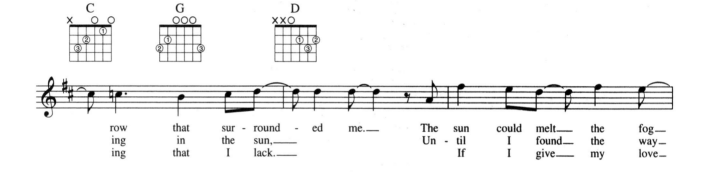

row that sur - round - ed me.___ The sun could melt___ the fog
ing in the sun,___ Un - til I found the way___
ing that I lack.___ If I give___ my love___

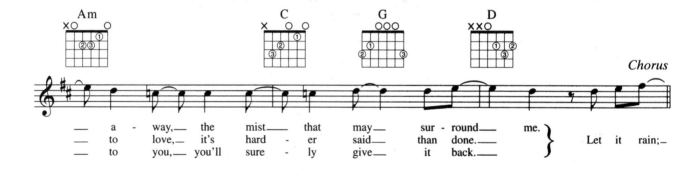

Chorus

___ a - way,___ the mist___ that may___ sur - round___ me.} Let it rain;___
___ to love,___ it's hard - er said___ than done.___
___ to you, you'll sure - ly give___ it back.___

___ let it rain.___ Let your love___ rain down on me.___

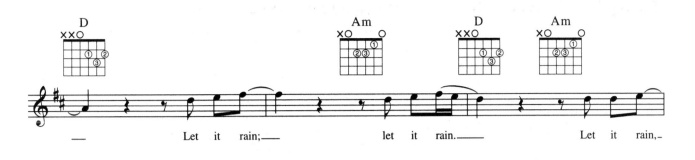

Let it rain;___ let it rain.___ Let it rain,___

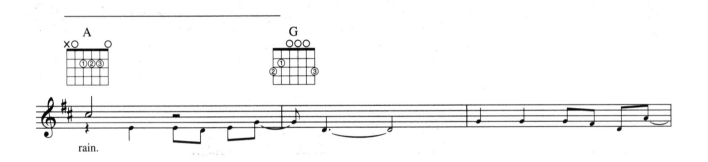

___ rain, rain.___ 2. My ___ rain,

rain.

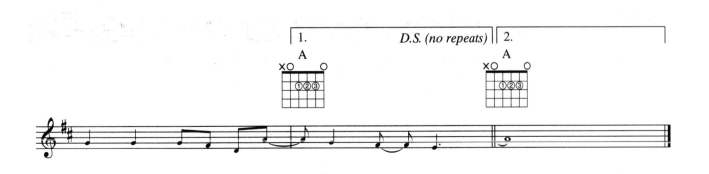

Lucky Man   Greg Lake

Scarborough Fair Traditional

Arpeggio T i m r m i
1 & 2 & 3 &

With movement

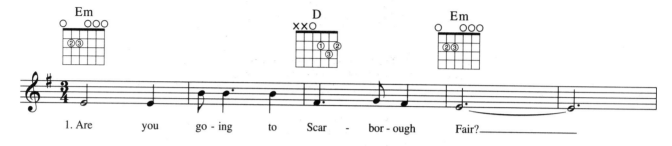

1. Are you go - ing to Scar - bor - ough Fair?_____

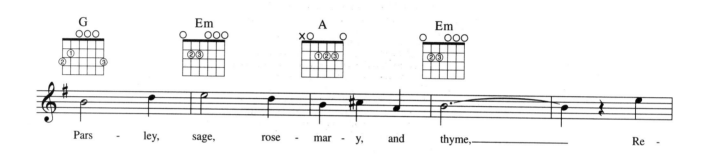

Pars - ley, sage, rose - mar - y, and thyme,_____ Re -

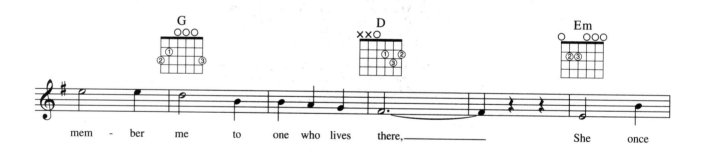

mem - ber me to one who lives there,_____ She once

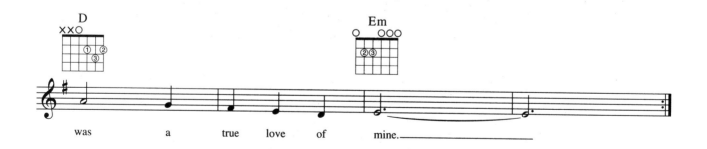

was a true love of mine._____

54

2. Tell her to make me a cambric shirt,
   Parsley, sage, rosemary, and thyme,
   Without no seam nor fine needlework,
   And then she'll be a true love of mine.

3. Tell her to wash it in yonder dry well,
   Parsley, sage, rosemary, and thyme,
   Which never sprung water nor rain ever fell,
   And then she'll be a true love of mine.

4. Tell her to dry it on yonder thorn,
   Parsley, sage, rosemary, and thyme,
   Which never bore blossom since Adam was born,
   And then she'll be a true love of mine.

5. Ask her to do me this courtesy,
   Parsley, sage, rosemary, and thyme,
   And ask for a like favor from me,
   And then she'll be a true love of mine.

6. Have you been Scarborough Fair?
   Parsley, sage, rosemary, and thyme,
   Remember me from one who lives there,
   For he once was a true love of mine.

7. Ask him to find me an acre of land,
   Parsley, sage, rosemary, and thyme,
   Between the salt water and the sea-sand,
   For then he'll be a true love of mine.

8. Ask him to plow it with a sheep's horn,
   Parsley, sage, rosemary, and thyme,
   And sow it all over with one peppercorn,
   For then he'll be a true love of mine.

9. Ask him to reap it with a sickle of leather,
   Parsley, sage, rosemary, and thyme,
   And gather it up with a rope made of heather,
   For then he'll be a true love of mine.

10. When he has done and finished his work,
    Parsley, sage, rosemary, and thyme,
    Ask him to come for his cambric shirt,
    For then he'll be a true love of mine.

11. If you say that you can't, then I shall reply,
    Parsley, sage, rosemary, and thyme,
    Oh, let me know that at least you will try,
    Or you'll never be a true love of mine.

The Tide Is High

John Holt, Tyrone Evans and Howard Barrett

The Times They Are A-Changin' Bob Dylan

Arpeggio T i m r m i
1 & 2 & 3 &

Moderately

1. Come gath - er 'round peo - ple where - ev - er you roam,_____ And ad - mit that the wa - ters a - round you have grown, And ac - cept it that soon you'll be drenched to the bone._____ If your time to you is worth sav - in'_____ Then you bet - ter start swim - min' or you'll

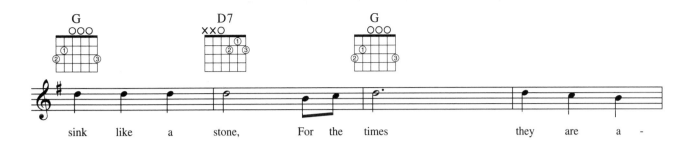

sink   like   a   stone,   For   the   times   they   are   a -

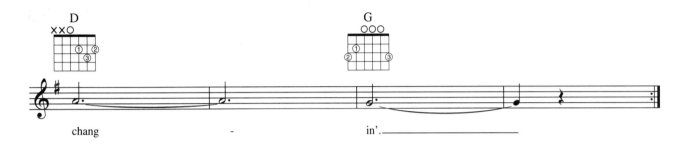

chang   -   in'. _____

2. Come writers and critics who prophesize with your pen,
   And keep your eyes wide, the chance won't come again,
   And don't speak too soon, for the wheel's still in spin,
   And there's no tellin' who that it's namin'.
   For the loser now will be later to win,
   For the times they are a-changin'.

3. Come senators, congressmen, please heed the call.
   Don't stand in the doorway, don't block up the hall.
   For he that gets hurt will be he who has stalled;
   There's battle outside and it is ragin'.
   It'll soon shake your windows and rattle your walls,
   For the times they are a-changin'.

4. Come mothers and fathers throughout the land,
   And don't criticize what you can't understand.
   Your sons and your daughters are beyond your command;
   Your old road is rapidly agin'.
   Please get out of the new one if you can't lend your hand,
   For the times they are a-changin'.

5. The line it is drawn, the curse it is cast.
   The slow one now will later be fast;
   As the present now will later be past;
   The order is rapidly fadin'.
   And the first one now will later be last,
   For the times they are a-changin'.

Mother and Child Reunion

Paul Simon

Strumming style ↓ ↑ ↓ ↑ ↑ ↓ ↑
1 & 2 &(3) & 4 &

Fast

No, I would not give— you false— hope on this strange and mourn - ful

day.— But the moth - er and child— re - un - ion— is

on - ly a mo-tion a - way, oh,— lit - tle dar - ling of mine.—

1. I can't for the life of me— re - mem - ber a
2. I just can't be - lieve it's so,— and though it seems

sad - der day   I know they say   let it be,—
strange to say.   I nev - er been laid   so low—

But it just don't work out that way,   And the course of a
in— such a mys - te - ri - ous way,—   And the course of a

Johnny Has Gone for a Soldier Traditional

Arpeggio T i m r T i m r
1 & 2 & 3 & 4 &

Slowly

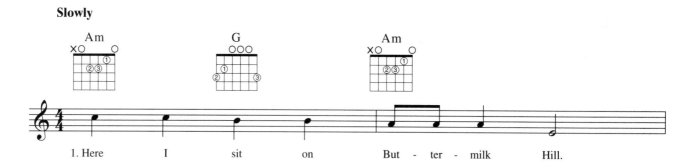

1. Here   I   sit   on   But - ter - milk   Hill.

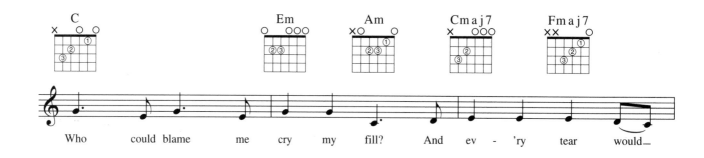

Who   could blame   me   cry   my   fill?   And   ev - 'ry   tear   would—

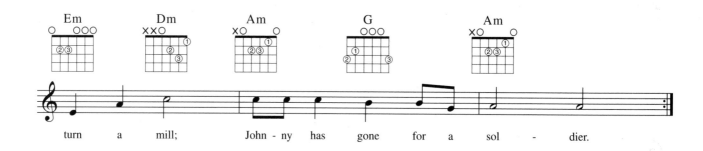

turn   a   mill;   John - ny   has   gone   for   a   sol - dier.

2. Me, oh my, I loved him so,
Broke my heart to see him go,
And only time will heal my woe;
Johnny has gone for a soldier.

3. I'll sell my rod, I'll sell my reel,
Likewise I'll sell my spinning wheel,
And buy my love a sword of steel;
Johnny has gone for a soldier.

4. I'll dye my dress, I'll dye it red,
And through the streets I'll beg for bread,
For the lad that I love from me has fled;
Johnny has gone for a soldier.

The Sound of Silence   Paul Simon

Arpeggio T i m r T i m r
1 & 2 & 3 & 4 &

Moderately

1. Hel - lo dark - ness, my old friend,
2. In rest - less dreams I walked a - lone,

I've come to talk with you a - gain,
nar - row streets of cob - ble - stone,

Be - cause a vi - sion soft - ly—
'Neath the ha - lo of a—

— creep - ing,— Left its seeds while I was sleep - ing,—
— street lamp,— I turned my col - lar to the cold and damp,—

And a vi - sion that was plant - ed in my
When my eyes were stabbed by the flash of a ne - on

brain still re - mains with - in the sound of si - lence.—
light that split the night and touched the sound of si - lence.—

3. And in the nak - ed light I saw ten thou-sand peo - ple, may - be

more.   Peo - ple talk - ing with - out____ speak - ing,____

Peo - ple hear - ing with - out____ list - 'ning,____   Peo - ple writ - ing

songs   that voi - ces nev - er share, and no one dare

dis - turb the sound of si - lence.____

4. "Fools" said I, "You do not know   si - lence like a can - cer

grows."   "Hear my words that I might____ teach you,____

Take my arms that I might____ reach you."____   But my

Greensleeves   Traditional

Arpeggio T i m r m i
1 & 2 & 3 &

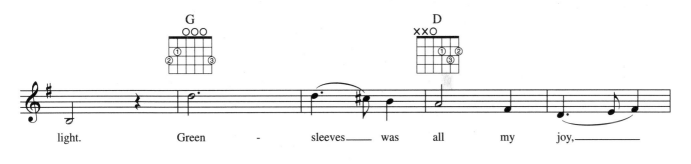

light.   Green - sleeves——was all my joy,——

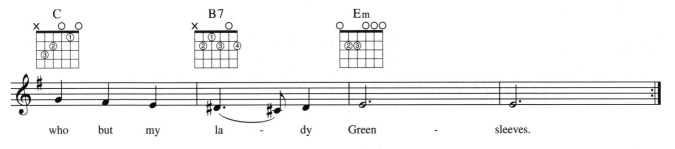

who but my la - dy Green - sleeves.

2. Your vows you've broken, like my heart,
Oh, why did you so enrapture me?
Now I remain in a world apart
But my heart remains in captivity.
Chorus

3. I have been ready at your hand,
To grant whatever you would crave,
I have both wagered life and land,
Your love and good-will for to have.
Chorus

4. If you intend thus to disdain,
It does the more enrapture me,
And even so, I still remain
A lover in captivity.
Chorus

5. My men were clothed all in green,
And they did ever wait on thee;
All this was gallant to be seen,
And yet thou wouldst not love me.
Chorus

6. Thou couldst desire no earthly thing,
But still thou hadst it readily.
Thy music still to play and sing;
And yet thou wouldst not love me.
Chorus

7. Well, I will pray to God on high,
That thou my constancy mayst see,
And that yet once before I die,
Thou wilt vouchsafe to love me.
Chorus

8. Ah, Greensleeves, now farewell, adieu,
To God I pray to prosper thee,
For I am still thy lover true,
Come once again and love me.
Chorus

Turn! Turn! Turn!
(To Everything There Is a Season)

Words from the Book of Ecclesiastes
Adaptation and Music by Pete Seeger

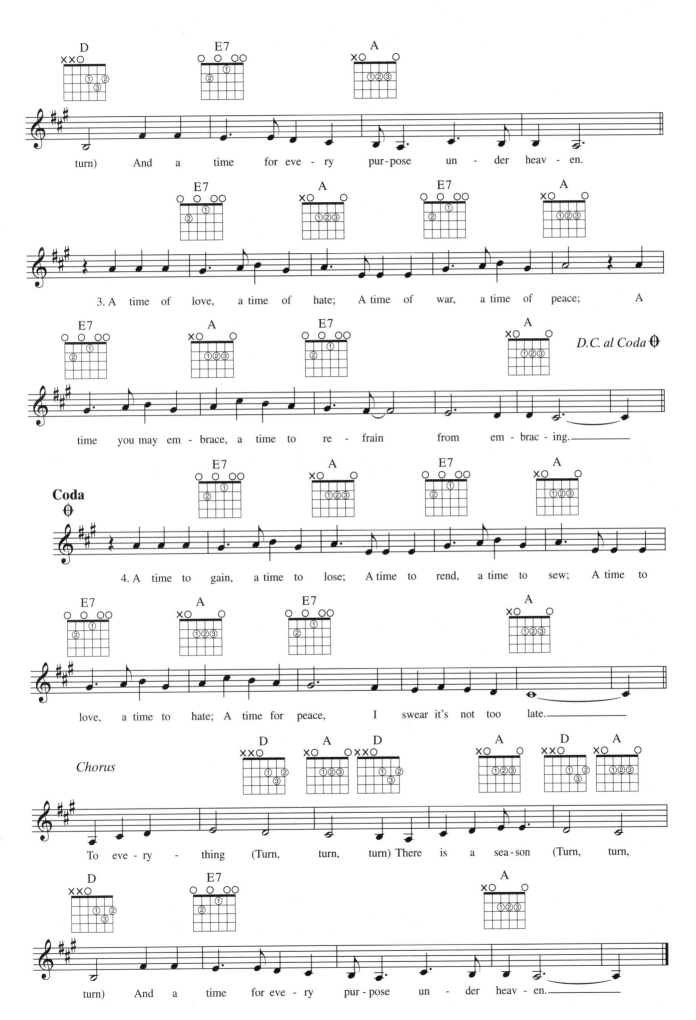

Two Tickets to Paradise Eddie Money

Bass-strum style **T ↓ T ↑ ↓**
　　　　　　　 1 2 3 & 4

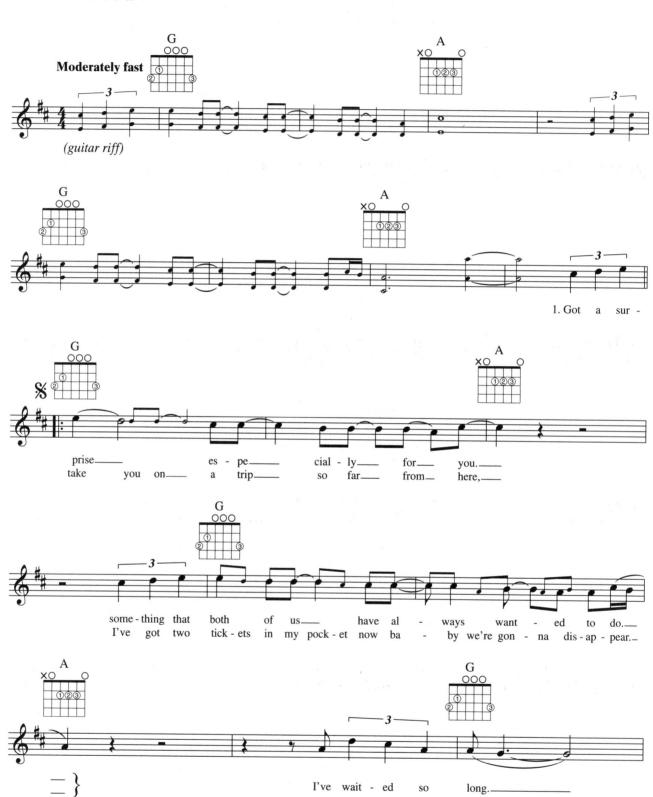

Moderately fast

(guitar riff)

1. Got a sur -

prise_____ es - pe_____ cial - ly_____ for_____ you._____
take you on_____ a trip_____ so far_____ from_____ here,_____

some - thing that both of us_____ have al - ways want - ed to do.
I've got two tick - ets in my pock - et now ba - by we're gon - na dis - ap - pear._____

I've wait - ed so long._____

A Horse with No Name

Dewey Bunnell

Strumming style ↓↓ ↑↓↑↓↑ ↑ ↑↓↑
1 2 (3)& 4 & 1 &(2) &(3) & 4 &

1. On the first part of the jour - ney I was
(3.) nine days_____ I let the horse run free 'cause the -

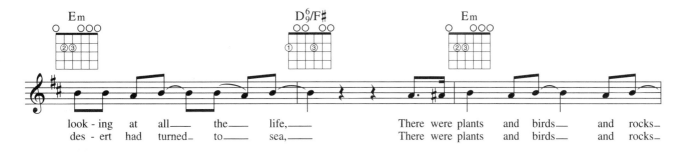

look - ing at all___ the___ life,___ There were plants and birds___ and rocks___
des - ert had turned___ to___ sea,___ There were plants and birds___ and rocks___

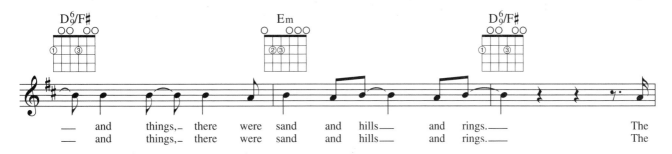

___ and things,___ there were sand and hills___ and rings.___ The
___ and things,___ there were sand and hills___ and rings.___ The

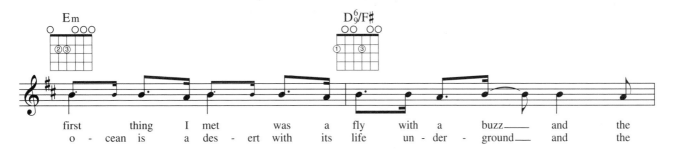

first thing I met was a fly with a buzz___ and the
o - cean is a des - ert with its life un - der - ground___ and the

sky with no___ clouds,___ The heat was hot___ and the
per - fect dis - guise___ a - bove.___ Un - der the cit - ies___ lies a

ground was dry,___ but the air was full___ of___ sound.
heart made of ground,___ but the hu - mans will give___ no___ love.

___ I've been through the des - ert on a horse with no name,___ It felt
You see I've

good to be out___ of the rain,___ In the des - ert___ you can re-

to Coda

mem - ber your name___ 'Cause there ain't no one for to give you no pain.___ La,

1. **2.**

la la la la la la la la la la.___ La ___ 2. Af - ter

two - days in the des - ert sun___ my skin be - gan___ to turn red, Af - ter

three days in the des - ert fun___ I was look - ing at a riv - er___ bed.

The Complete Guitar Player Songbook

Book 2

by Russ Shipton

78   I Am a Rock
80   Be Thankful for What You've Got
82   Father and Son
85   If Not for You
88   Maggie May
90   Wonderful Tonight
92   Woodstock
94   Both Sides Now
96   I'll Be
99   Oh, Pretty Woman
102   Morning Has Broken
103   Candle in the Wind
106   It Ain't Me Babe
108   The Boxer
112   Can You Feel the Love Tonight
114   House of the Rising Sun
115   All along the Watchtower
118   Chelsea Morning

120   Homeward Bound
122   La Bamba
125   That's How Strong My Love Is
128   Lemon Tree
130   Superstar
132   I Want You
134   Behind Blue Eyes
137   Tainted Love
140   Leaving on a Jet Plane
142   Puff the Magic Dragon
144   Rainy Day Women #12 & 35
146   Teach Your Children
148   Wild World
150   Take Me Home, Country Roads
153   Hard Headed Woman
156   Fly Me to the Moon
157   Tonight I'll Be Staying Here with You
160   Mrs. Robinson

Amsco Publications
A Part of **The Music Sales Group**
New York/London/Paris/Sydney/Copenhagen/Berlin/Tokyo/Madrid

I Am a Rock Paul Simon

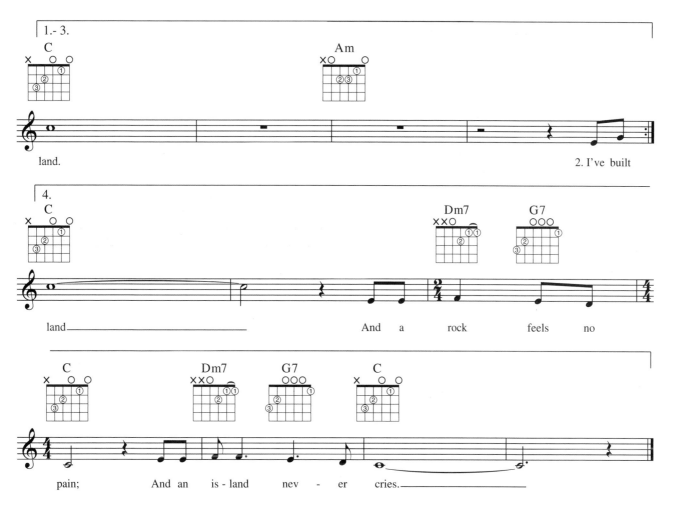

1.- 3.

| C | | | | Am |

land.

2. I've built

4.

| C | | | Dm7 | G7 |

land_____ And a rock feels no

| C | Dm7 | G7 | C |

pain; And an is - land nev - er cries._____

2. I've built walls.
A fortress deep and mighty,
That none may penetrate.
I have no need of friendship; friendship causes pain.
It's laughter and it's loving I disdain.
I am a rock,
I am an island.

3. Don't talk of love,
But I've heard the words before;
It's sleeping in my memory.
I won't disturb the slumber of feelings that have died.
If I never loved I never would have cried.
I am a rock,
I am an island.

4. I have my books
And my poetry to protect me;
I am shielded in my armor,
Hiding in my room, safe within my womb.
I touch no one and no one touches me.
I am a rock,
I am an island.
And a rock feels no pain;
And an island never cries.

Be Thankful for What You've Got

William DeVaughn

Strumming style ↓ ↓ ↓ ↑ ↓ ↑
1 2 3 & 4 &

Moderately slow, with a beat

Though you may not drive a great big Cad - il - lac,

gots the white - walls,___ T. V. an - ten - nas___ in the

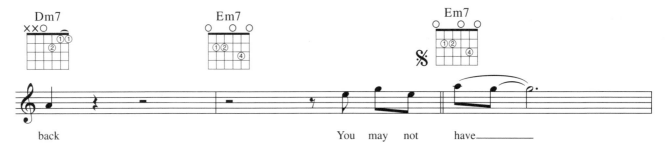

back You may not have___

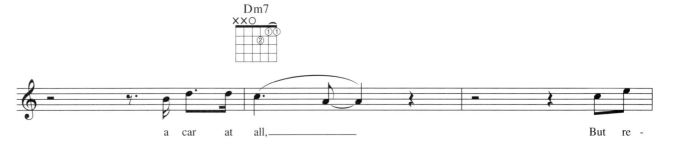

a car at all,___ But re -

mem - ber, broth - ers and sis - ters, you can still___ stand tall.___

Father and Son   Cat Stevens

Bass-strum style T ↓ T ↑ ↓ ↑
1 2 3 & 4 &

It's   not   time   to make a change,   just   re - lax,   take   it
It's   not   time   to make a change,   just   sit   down,   take   it

eas - y,   You're   still   young,   that's   your   fault,   There's   so   much   you   have   to
slow - ly,   You're   still   young,   that's   your   fault,   There's   so   much   you   have—   to   go

know.
through.   }   Find   a   girl,   set - tle   down,   if   you   want,   you   can

mar - ry,   Look   at   me: I   am   old,   but   I'm   hap - py.

{ I   was   once like   you   are   now,   and   I   know   that   it's   not
{ All   the   times—   that   I've   cried,   keep-in'   all   the   things   I

If Not for You   Bob Dylan

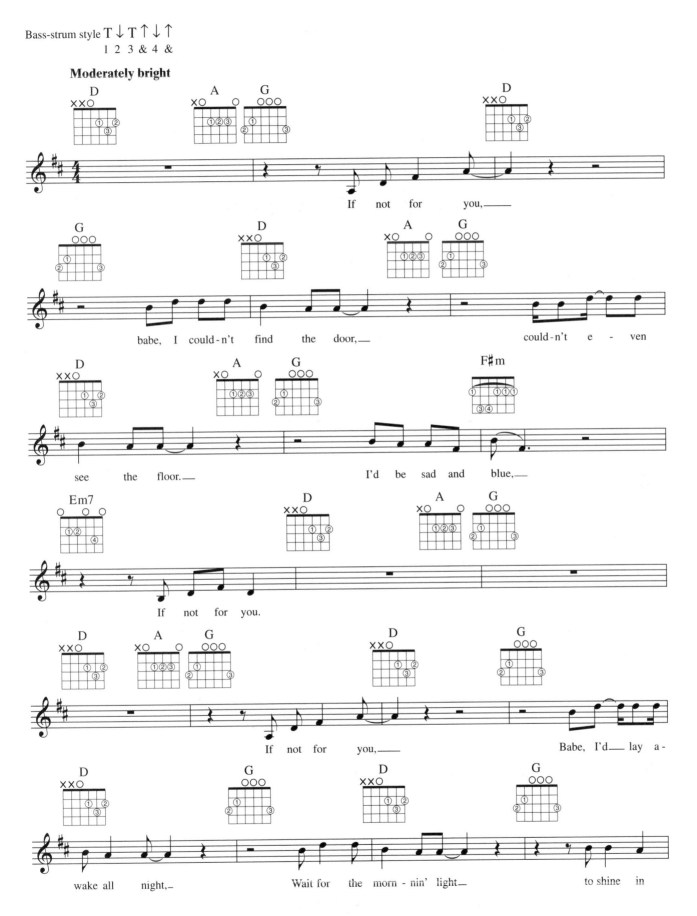

Maggie May

Rod Stewart and Martin Quittenton

Alternating thumb style
T T i T m T
1 2 & 3 & 4

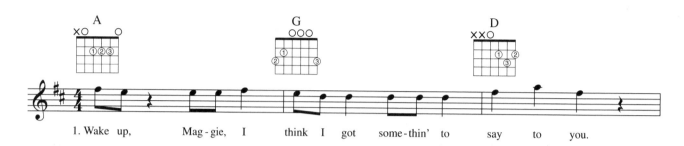

1. Wake up, Mag - gie, I think I got some - thin' to say to you.

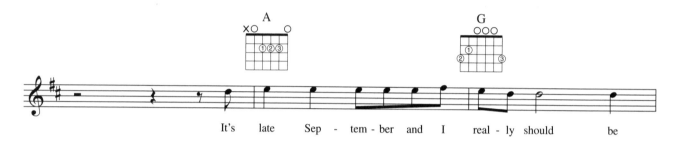

It's late Sep - tem - ber and I real - ly should be

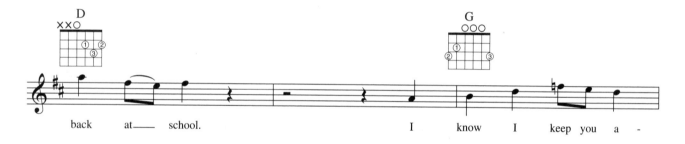

back at school. I know I keep you a -

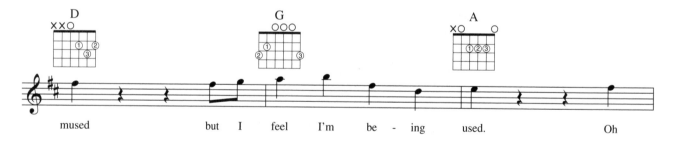

mused but I feel I'm be - ing used. Oh

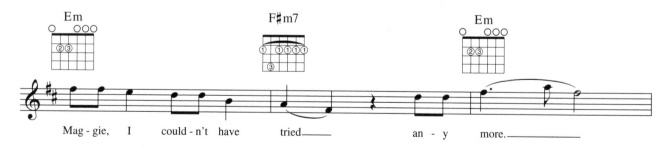

Mag - gie, I could - n't have tried an - y more.

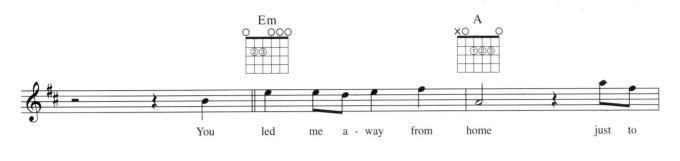

You led me a - way from home just to

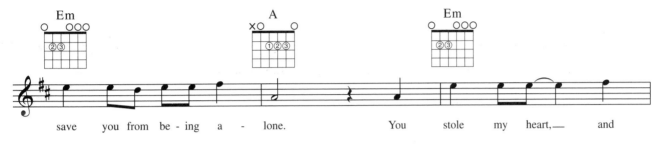

save you from be - ing a - lone. You stole my heart,— and

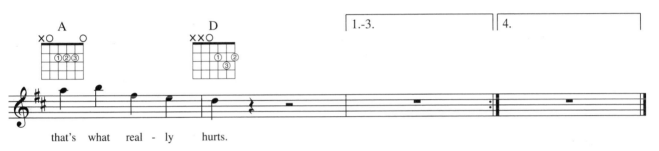

that's what real - ly hurts.

2. The morning sun when it's in your face really shows your age.
But that don't worry me none in my eyes you're everything.
I laughed at all of your jokes, my love you didn't need to coax.
Oh, Maggie I couldn't have tried any more.
You lured me away from home, just to save you from being alone.
You stole my soul, and that's a pain I can do without.

3. All I needed was a friend to lend a guiding hand.
But you turned into a lover and
Mother what a lover, you wore me out.
All you did was wreck my bed,
And in the morning kick me in the head.
Oh Maggie I couldn't have tried anymore.
You lured me away from home 'cause you didn't want to be alone.
You stole my heart, I couldn't leave you if I tried.

4. I suppose I could collect my books and get on back to school.
Or steal my daddy's cue and make a living out of playing pool.
Or find myself a rock and roll band that needs a helpin' hand.
Oh Maggie I wish I'd never seen your face.
You made a first-class fool out of me,
But I'm as blind as a fool can be.
You stole my heart, but I love you anyway.

Wonderful Tonight

Eric Clapton

Arpeggio T i T m i r m i
1 & 2 & 3 & 4 &

1. It's late in the eve - ning; she's won - d'ring what

clothes to wear.__ She puts on her make - up

and brush - es her long blonde hair__ And then__ she

asks me, "Do I look all right?" And I say "Yes, you look

to Coda ⊕ 1.

won - der - ful to - night."

2.
night." I feel won - der - ful— be - cause I see— the love light in— your eyes. And the won - der of it all— is that you just don't re - al - ize how much— I

D.S. al Coda

love you.

Coda
night." Oh, my dar - ling, you were won - der - ful to -

night.

2. We go to a party, and everyone turns to see
   This beautiful lady that's walking around with me.
   And then she asks me, "Do you feel all right?"
   And I say, "Yes, I feel wonderful tonight."

3. It's time to go home now, and I've got an achin' head,
   So I give her the car keys, and she helps me to bed.
   And then I tell her, as I turn out the light,
   I say, "My darlin', you were wonderful tonight."
   Oh, my darling, you were wonderful tonight.

Woodstock   Joni Mitchell

Strumming style/half bar stress

↓ ↓ ↑   ↑ ↓
1 2 & (3) & 4

1. I came up-on___ a child___ of God,___ he was walk-ing a-long___ the

road and I asked him, "Where are you go - ing?"___ This is told

me: "I'm go-ing on down___ to Yas - gur's farm,___ gon - na

join in a rock___ and roll band.___ I'm gon-na camp out___ on the

Chorus

land and try 'n' get___ my soul___ free."___ We are

2. Then can I walk beside you
   I have come here to lose the smog
   I feel just like a cog
   In something turning
   Well maybe it's the time of year
   Or maybe it's the time of man
   I don't know who I am
   But life is for learning
   Chorus

3. By the time I got to Woodstock
   They were half a million strong
   Everywhere there was song and celebration
   I dreamed I saw the bombers
   Riding shotgun in the sky
   Turning into butterflies above our nation
   Chorus

Both Sides Now   Joni Mitchell

Strumming style ↑ ↓ ↑ ↓ ↑ ↓ ↑ ↓
1 & 2 & 3 & 4 &

Moderately

1. Bows and flows of an-gel hair,— And ice-cream cas-tles in the air,— And

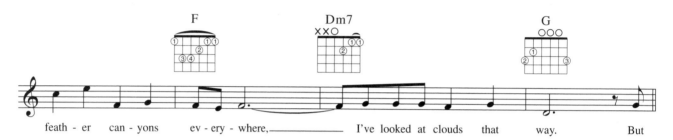

feath-er can-yons ev-ery-where,————— I've looked at clouds that way. But

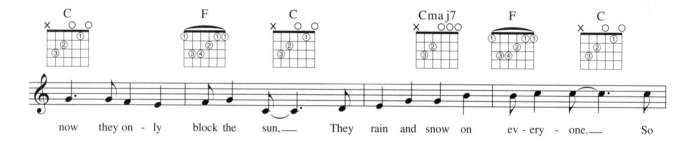

now they on-ly block the sun,— They rain and snow on ev-ery-one.— So

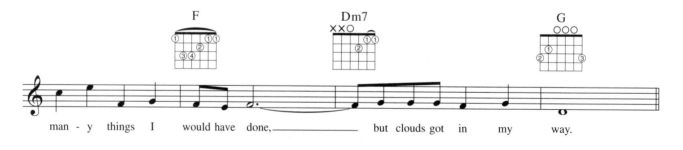

man-y things I would have done,————— but clouds got in my way.

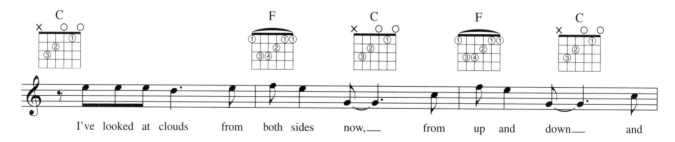

I've looked at clouds from both sides now,— from up and down— and

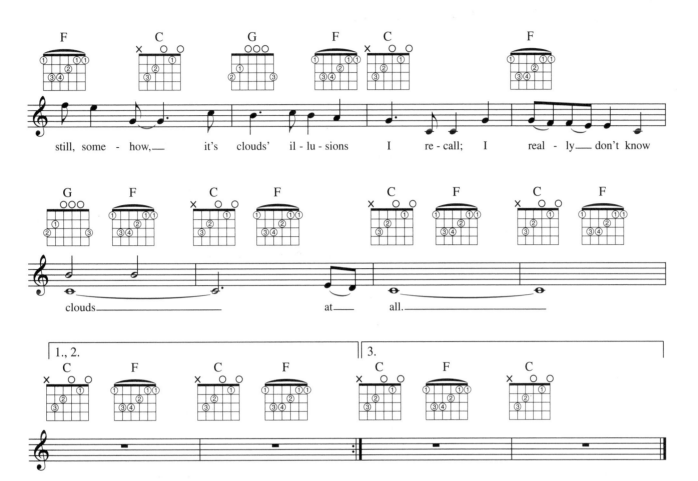

still, some - how,—   it's clouds' il - lu - sions   I   re - call;   I   real - ly— don't know

clouds—   at—   all.—

1., 2.   3.

2. Moons and Junes and ferris wheels,
   The dizzy dancing way you feel
   As every fairy tale comes real,
   I've looked at love that way.

   But now it's just another show,
   You leave 'em laughing when you go,
   And if you care, don't let them know,
   Don't give yourself away.

   I've looked at love from both sides now,
   From give and take and still, somehow,
   It's love's illusions I recall,
   I really don't know love at all.

3. Tears and fears and feeling proud,
   To say "I love you" right out loud,
   Dreams and schemes and circus crowds,
   I've looked at life that way.

   Oh but now old friends they're acting strange,
   They shake their heads, they say I've changed
   Well something's lost, but something's gained
   In living every day.

   I've looked at life from both sides now
   From win and lose and still somehow
   It's life's illusions I recall,
   I really don't know life at all.

I'll Be
Edwin McCain

gal - lows of heart - ache_ that hang from a - bove._

_ I'll be your cry - in'

shoul - der, I'll_ be love su - i - cide._ And

I'll be bet - ter when I'm old - er, I'll_

be the great - est fan of your life._

to Coda

D.S. al Coda

2. And

Coda

And I've_ dropped out, I've burned up. I fought my way

Oh, Pretty Woman

Roy Orbison and Bill Dees

Bass-strum style T ↓ T ↑ ↓ ↑
1 2 3 & 4 &

Moderately

Pret - ty   Wom - an,____   walk - ing   down   the   street,____   Pret - ty

Wom - an,____   the   kind   I'd   like   to   meet.____   Pret - ty   Wom - an.____

I   don't   be - lieve   you,____   you're   not   the   truth.____   No   one   could

look   as   good   as   you._____   *Mer - cy.*____   Pret - ty

Wom - an,____   won't   you   par - don   me?____   Pret - ty   Wom - an,____   I   could - n't

help   but   see,____   Pret - ty   Wom - an,____   that   you   look   love - ly   as   can

be.   Are you lone - ly   just like me?

Pret - ty Wom - an stop a while,—   Pret - ty Wom - an talk a while,—

Pret - ty Wom - an give your smile to me—

Pret - ty Wom - an yeah, yeah, yeah.—   Pret - ty Wom - an look my way,—

Pret - ty Wom - an say you'll stay with me.—   'Cause I

need you,— I'll treat you right.   Come to me ba - by,—

— Be mine to - night.—   Pret - ty

D   Bm   D   Bm

Wom - an,— don't walk on by,— Pret - ty Wom - an,— don't make me cry,— Pret - ty

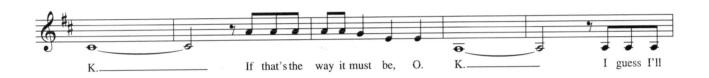

G   A7

Wom - an———————— don't walk a - way.— Hey,———————— O.

K.——————— If that's the way it must be, O. K.——————— I guess I'll

go on home,— it's late. There'll be to - mor - row night, but

wait! What do I see—————————————————————— Is she

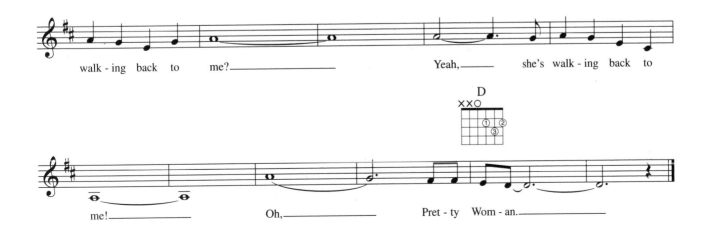

walk - ing back to me?——————— Yeah,——— she's walk - ing back to

D

me!——————— Oh,——— Pret - ty Wom - an.———————

Morning Has Broken

Words by Eleanor Farjeon
Musical arrangement by Cat Stevens

Bass-strum style T ↓ ↑ ↓
1 2 & 3

Moderately

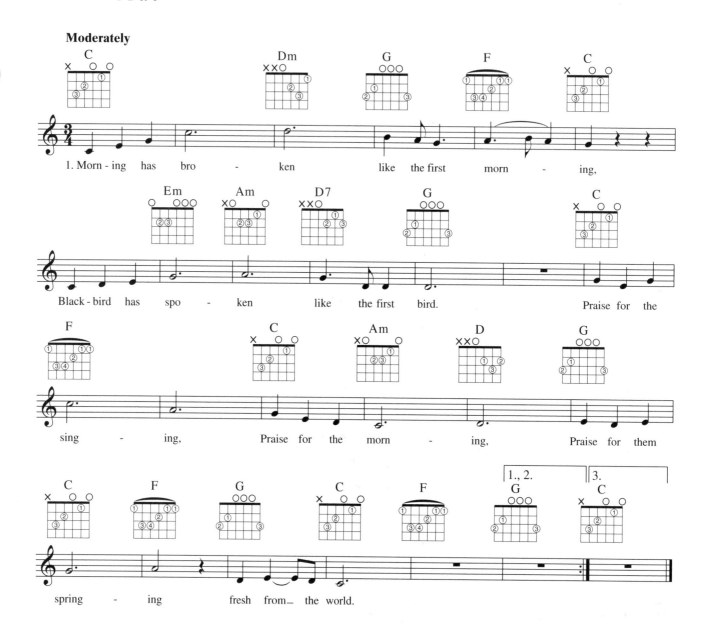

1. Morn - ing has bro - ken like the first morn - ing,

Black - bird has spo - ken like the first bird. Praise for the

sing - ing, Praise for the morn - ing, Praise for them

spring - ing fresh from— the world.

2. Sweet the rain's new fall, sunlit from heaven
   Like the first dewfall, on the first grass
   Praise for the sweetness of the wet garden
   Sprung in completeness where his feet pass

3. Mine is the sunlight, mine is the morning
   Born of the one light, Eden saw play
   Praise with elation, praise every morning
   God's recreation of the new day

Candle in the Wind

Elton John & Bernie Taupin

Alternating thumb style
T T i T m T
1 2 & 3 & 4

Moderately slow

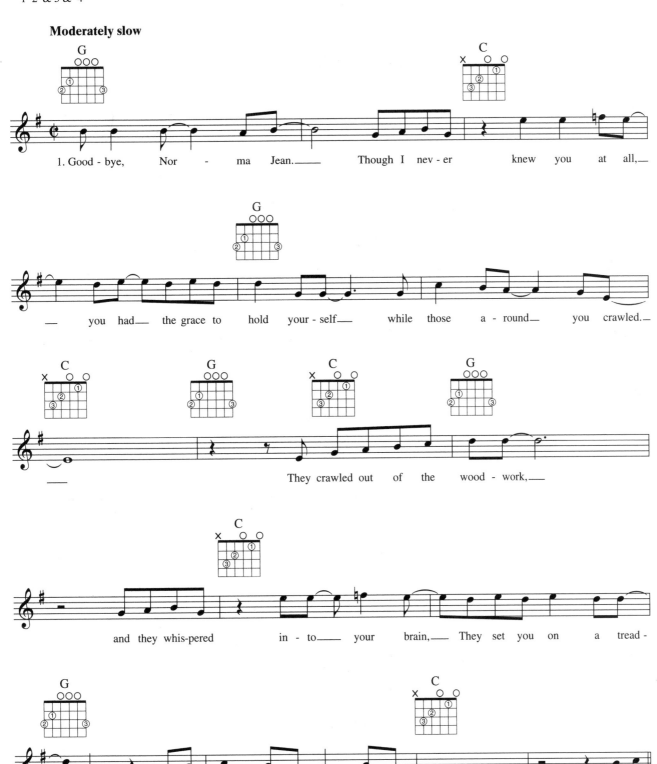

3. Good - bye, Nor - ma Jean._____ Though I nev - er
Good - bye, Nor - ma Jean_____ From the young man in the

knew you at all,_____ you had_____ the grace to
twen - ty - sec - ond row,_____ who sees_____ you as some - thing

hold your - self_____ while those a - round_____ you crawled.
more than sex - u - al,_____ More than those just our Mar - i - lyn Mon -

1.
_____

2.   *D.S. al Coda*
roe._____ And it

Coda
The can - dle had burned out long be - fore,_____ your

leg - end nev - er did.

2. Loneliness was tough,
   The toughest role you ever played.
   Hollywood created a superstar,
   And pain was the price you paid.
   Even when you died
   Oh the press still hounded you.
   All the papers had to say
   Was that Marilyn was found in the nude.
   Chorus

It Ain't Me Babe

Bob Dylan

Alternating thumb style
T T i T m T
1 2 & 3 & 4

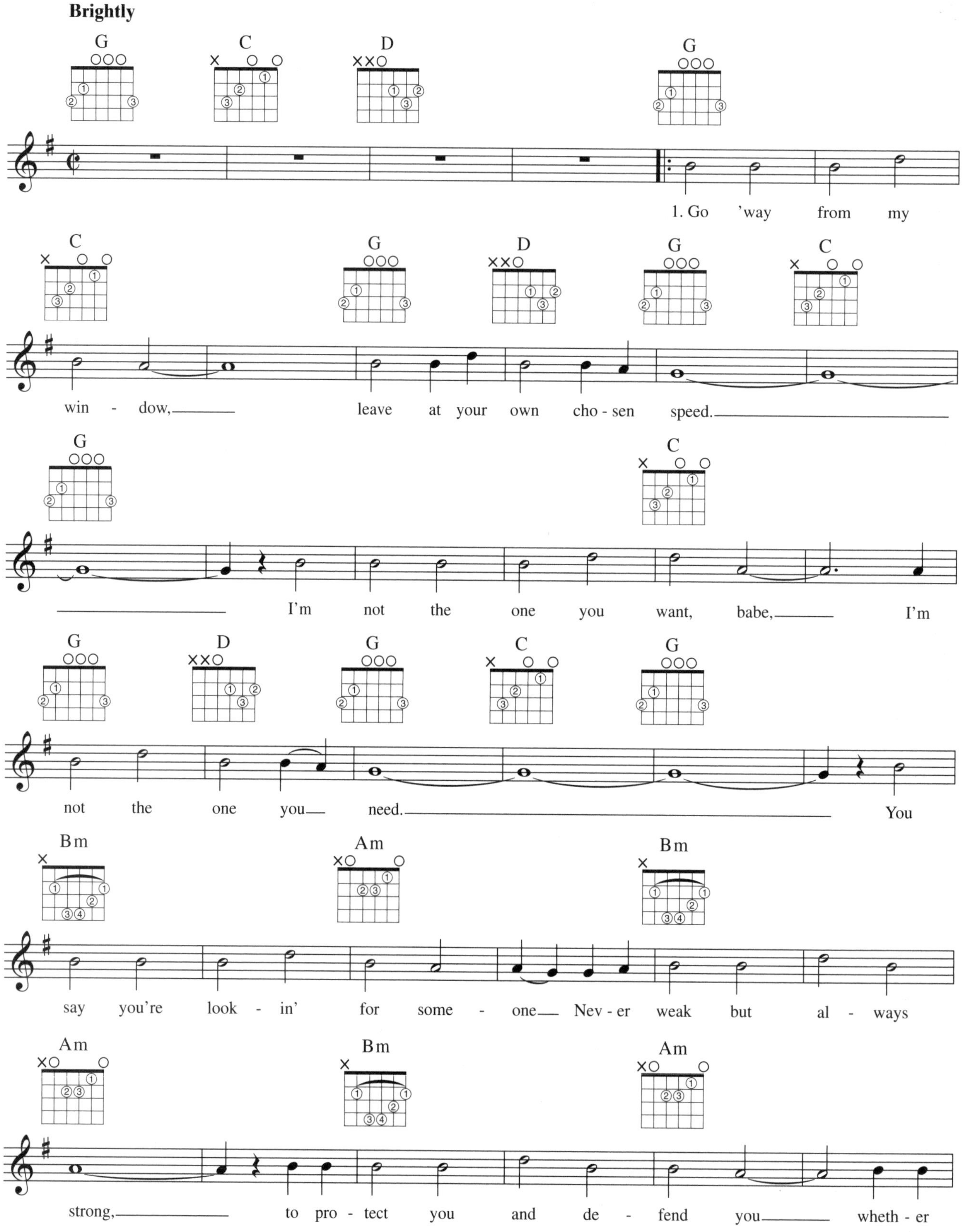

Brightly
G C D G
1. Go 'way from my
C G D G C
win - dow, leave at your own cho - sen speed.
G C
I'm not the one you want, babe, I'm
G D G C G
not the one you need. You
Bm Am Bm
say you're look - in' for some - one Nev - er weak but al - ways
Am Bm Am
strong, to pro - tect you and de - fend you wheth - er

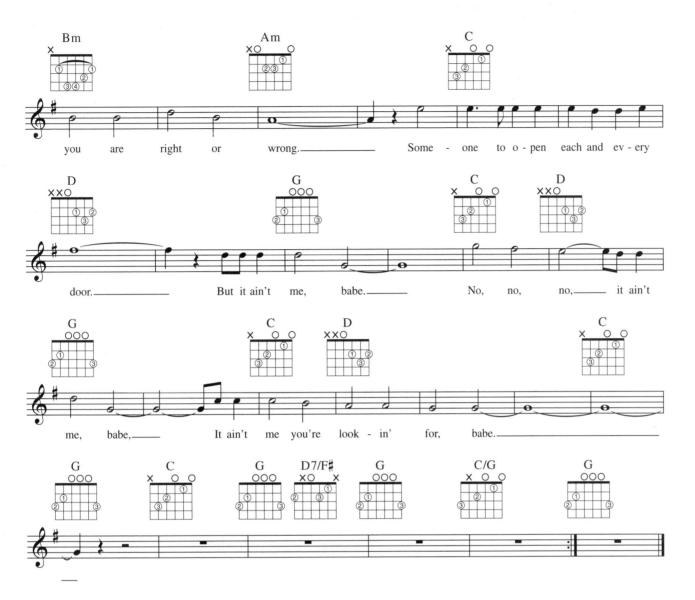

Bm   Am   C

you   are   right   or   wrong._____   Some - one   to o - pen   each and ev - ery

D   G   C   D

door._____   But it ain't   me,   babe._____   No,   no,   no,_____   it ain't

G   C   D   C

me,   babe,_____   It ain't   me you're   look - in'   for,   babe._____

G   C   G   D7/F♯   G   C/G   G

2. Go lightly from the ledge, babe,
   Go lightly on the ground.
   I'm not the one you want, babe,
   I will only let you down.
   You say you're lookin' for someone
   Who will promise never to part,
   Someone to close his eyes for you,
   Someone to close his heart,
   Someone who will die for you an' more,
   But it ain't me, babe,
   No, no, no, it ain't me, babe,
   It ain't me you're lookin' for, babe.

3. Go melt back into the night, babe,
   Everything inside is made of stone.
   There's nothing in here moving,
   An' anyway I'm not alone.
   You say you're looking for someone
   Who'll pick you up each time you fall,
   To gather flowers constantly
   An' to come each time you call,
   A lover for your life an' nothing more,
   But it ain't me, babe,
   No, no, no, it ain't me, babe,
   It ain't me you're lookin' for, babe.

The Boxer   Paul Simon

Alternating thumb style
T i T m T i T
1 & 2 & 3 & 4

Moderately

I am just a poor boy. Though my sto-ry's sel-dom told, I have squan-dered my re-

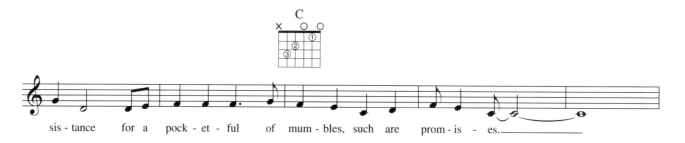

sis-tance for a pock-et-ful of mum-bles, such are prom-is-es.

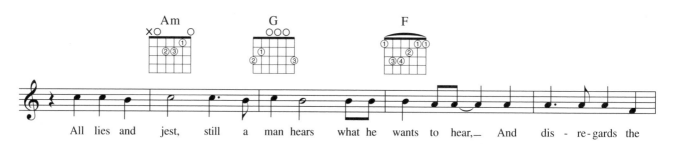

All lies and jest, still a man hears what he wants to hear,— And dis-re-gards the

rest.— When I left my home and my fam - i - ly,— I was

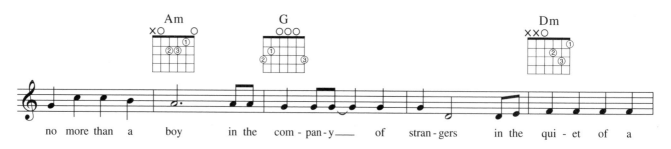

no more than a boy in the com-pan-y— of stran-gers in the qui-et of a

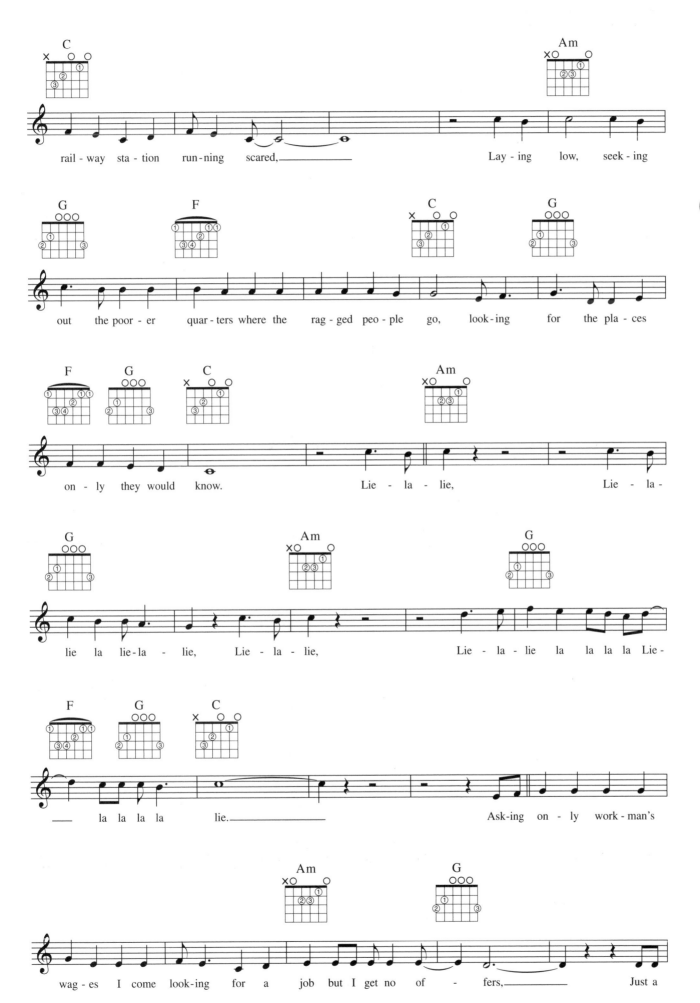

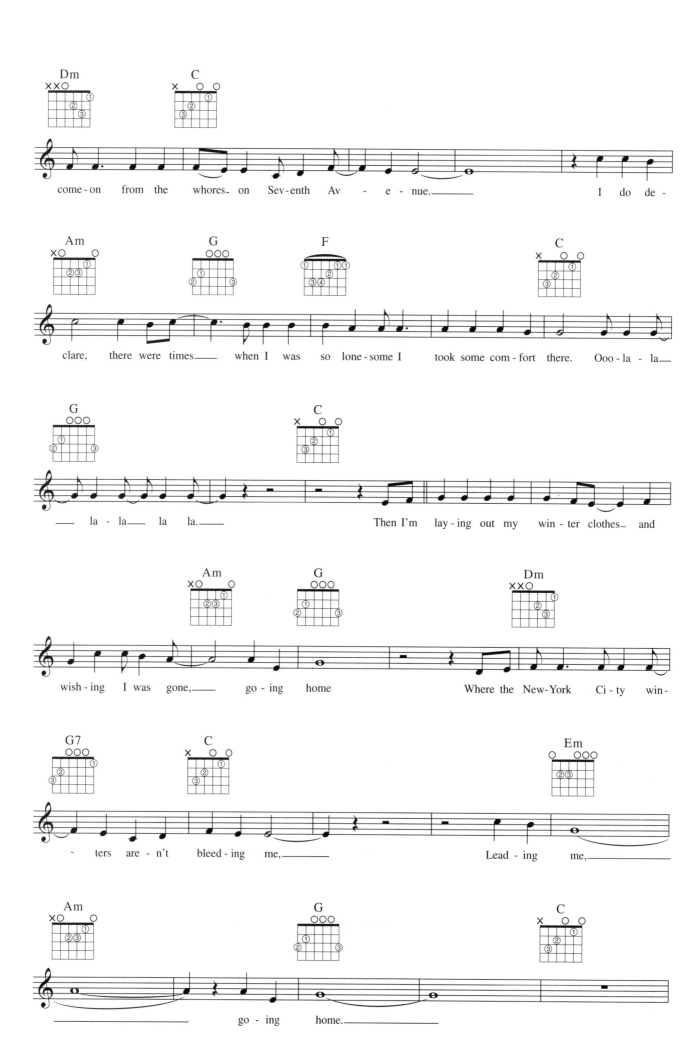

Can You Feel The Love Tonight

Music by Elton John
Lyrics by Tim Rice

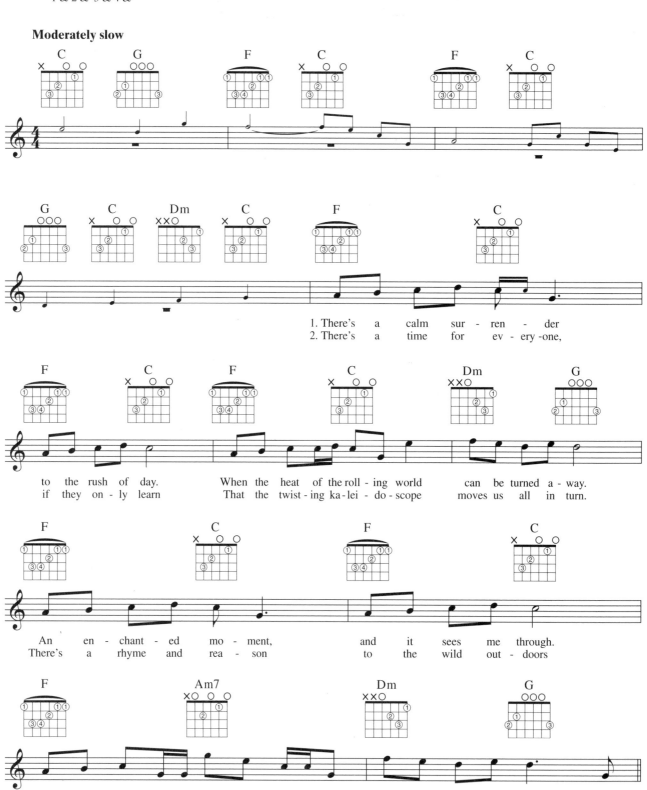

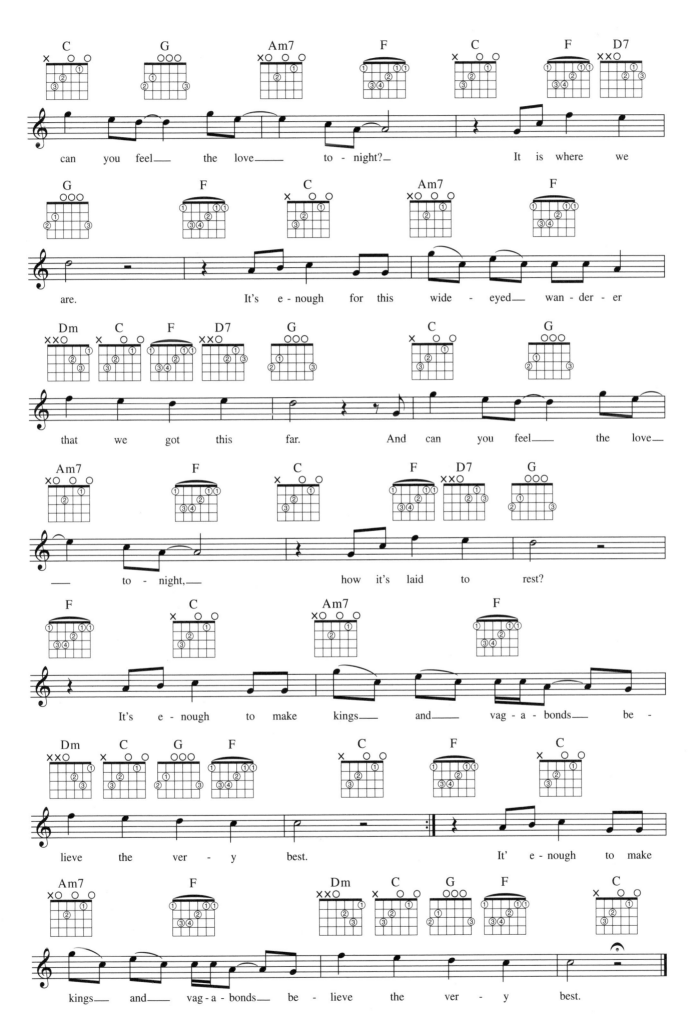

House of the Rising Sun   Traditional

Arpeggio T i m r m i
        1 2 3 4 5 6

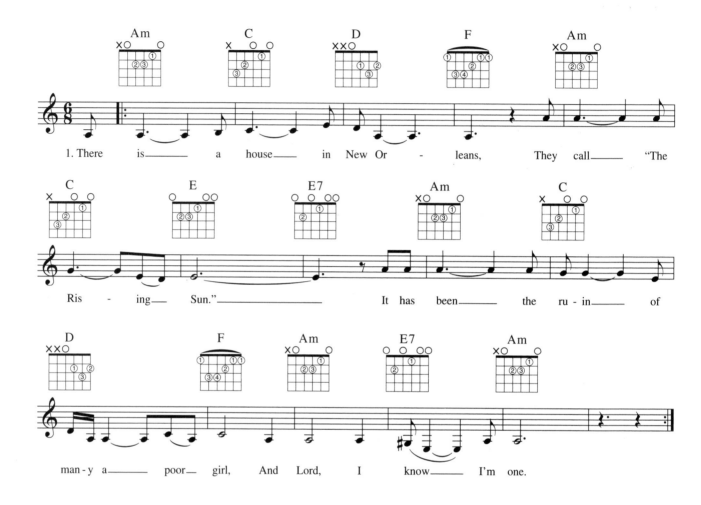

1. There   is_____   a   house_____   in   New Or   -   leans,   They   call_____   "The

Ris   -   ing___   Sun."_____   It   has   been_____   the   ru - in_____   of

man - y a_____   poor__   girl,   And   Lord,   I   know_____   I'm   one.

2. My mother, she's a tailor,
   She sells those new blue jeans.
   My sweetheart, he's a drunkard, Lord,
   Drinks down in New Orleans.

3. Go tell my baby sister
   Never do like I have done,
   To shun that house in New Orleans
   They call "The Rising Sun."

4. I'm going back to New Orleans,
   My race is almost run.
   Going back to end my life
   Beneath "The Rising Sun."

All along the Watchtower   Bob Dylan

Strumming style ↓ ↑ ↓ ↑ ↓ ↑ ↓ ↑
            1 & 2 & 3 & 4 &

Moderately

know what an-y of it is worth."_____

"No rea-son to get ex-cit-ed,"

the thief, he kind-ly spoke,___ "There are man-y here a-

mong us who feel that life is but a joke.

But, you and I, we've been through that, And this is not our fate,___

___ So, let us not talk false-ly now,

The hour is get-ting late."_____ All a-long the

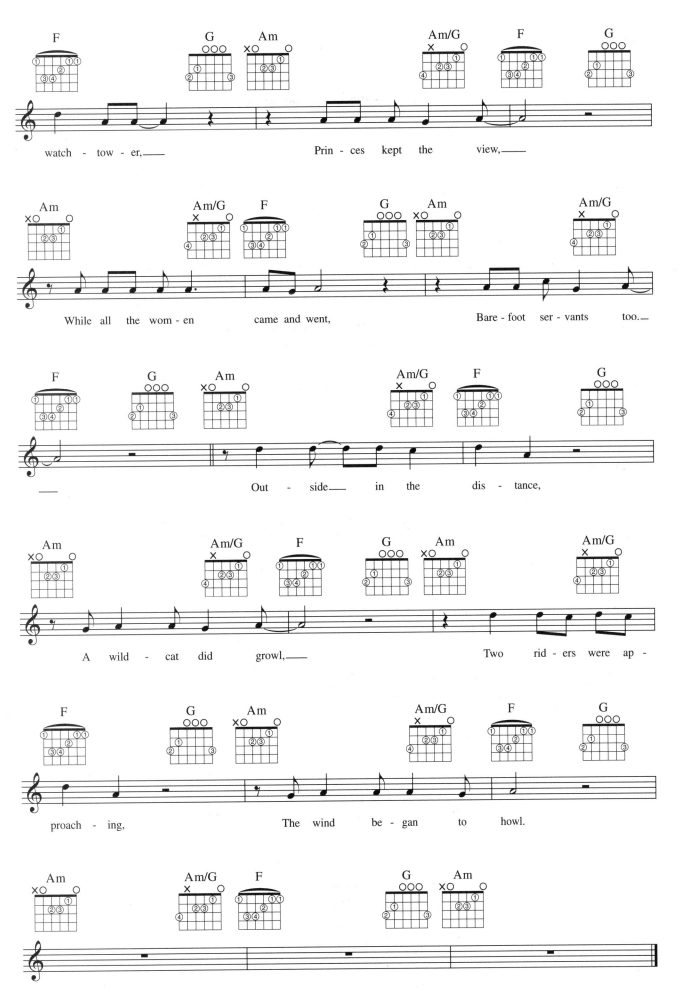

Chelsea Morning Joni Mitchell

Strumming style ↓ ↓ ↑   ↑ ↓ ↑
1 2 &(3) & 4 &

Introduction

1. Woke up,— it was a Chel-sea morn-ing and the first thing that I heard—
2. Woke up,— it was a Chel-sea morn-ing and the first thing that I saw—

— was the song out-side my win-dow,— and the traf-fic wrote the
— Was the sun through yel-low cur-tains— and a rain-bow on the

words. It came ring-ing up— like Christ-mas bells— and rap-ping up— like—
wall; Blue, red, green, and gold— to wel-come you— Crim-son crys-tal beads— to—

— pipes and— drums.— Oh, won't you stay? We'll
— beck-on.— Oh, won't you stay? We'll

118

put on the day__ and we'll wear it till__ the night comes.__
put on the day,__ There's a sun show eve - ry sec - ond.__

Now the cur - tain o - pens on a por - trait of to - day And the streets are paved with

pass - ers - by And pig - eons fly__ and pa - pers lie,__ Wait - ing to blow a - way.__

D.S. al Coda

Coda

stay.__ Pret - ty ba - by won't__ you Wake up,__ it's a

Chel - sea morn - ing.

3. Woke up, it was a Chelsea morning
And the first thing that I knew
There was milk and toast and honey
And a bowl of oranges, too;
And the sun poured in like butterscotch
And stuck to all my senses.

Oh, won't you stay?
We'll put on the day;
And we'll talk in present tenses.

When the curtain closes, and the rainbow runs away,
I will bring you incense
Owls by night, by candlelight,
By jewel-light,
If only you will stay.

Pretty baby, won't you
Wake up, it's Chelsea morning.

119

Homeward Bound   Paul Simon

Alternating thumb style
T i T m T i T
1 & 2 & 3 & 4

1. I'm sit-tin' in the rail-way sta-tion, got a tick-et for my

des - tin - a - tion.____ Mm____

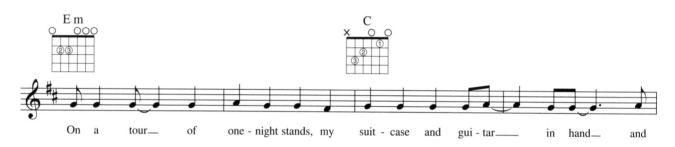

On a tour___ of one-night stands, my suit-case and gui-tar___ in hand___ and

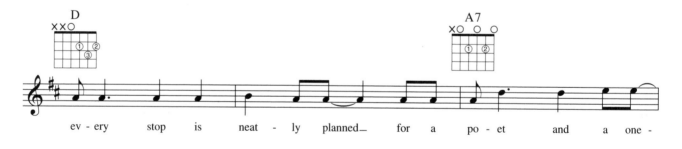

ev - ery stop is neat - ly planned___ for a po - et and a one -

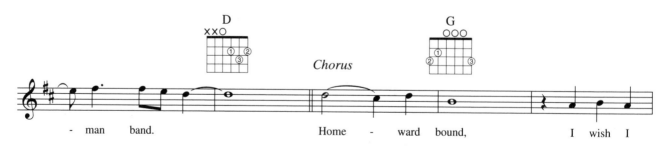

Chorus

- man band.   Home - ward bound,   I wish I

2. Every day's an endless stream
   Of cigarettes and magazines.
   And each town looks the same to me, the movies and the factories,
   And every stranger's face I see reminds me that I long to be
   Chorus

3. Tonight I'll sing my songs again,
   I'll play the game and pretend.
   But all my words come back to me in shades of mediocrity
   Like emptiness in harmony; I need someone to comfort me.
   Chorus

La Bamba   Mexican Traditional

Bass-strum style T ↓ T ↑ ↓ ↑
1 2 3 & 4 &

Moderately
Intro

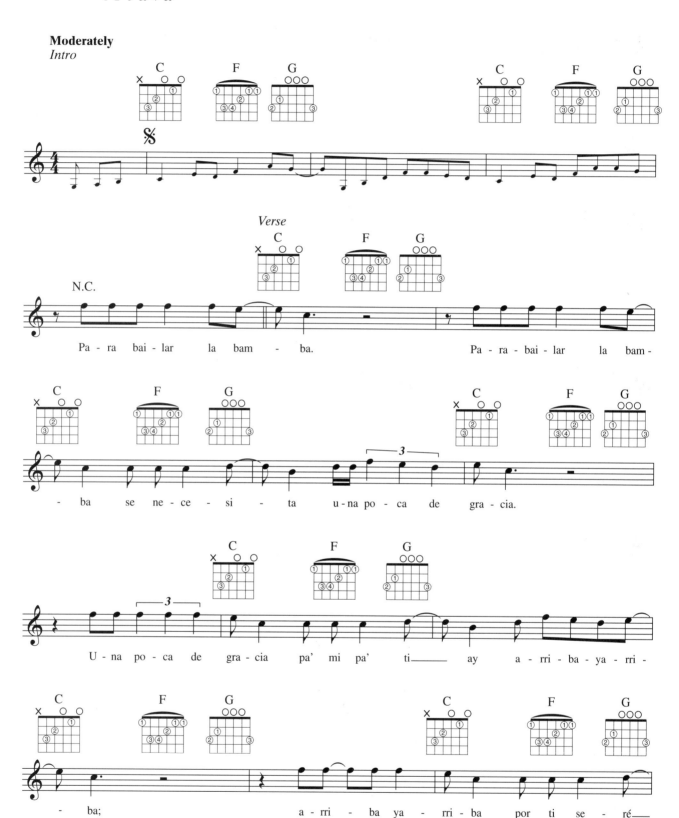

Pa - ra bai - lar la bam - ba. Pa - ra - bai - lar la bam-

Verse
N.C.

- ba se ne - ce - si - ta u - na po - ca de gra - cia.

U - na po - ca de gra - cia pa' mi pa' ti___ ay a - rri - ba - ya - rri-

- ba; a - rri - ba ya - rri - ba por ti se - ré___

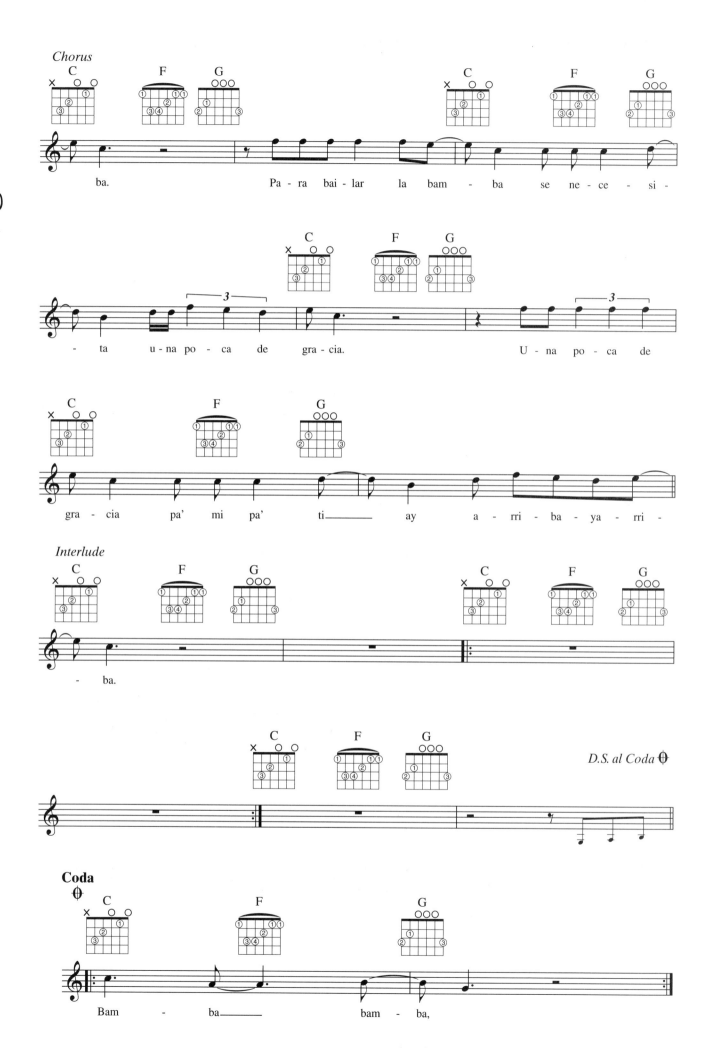

That's How Strong My Love Is
Roosevelt Jamison

Bass-strum style T ↓ ↑ ↓ T ↓ ↑ ↓
          1 2 & 3 4 5 & 6

Slowly, with a steady beat

1. If I was the south wind way up there I'd blow our love most

an - y - where. I'll be the moon when the sun goes down,

just to let you know that I'm still a-round. That's how strong

my love is, - whoa,_____ that's how strong my love__ is._____

That's how strong my love is, ba-by, ba-by, that's how strong

my love is.   2. I'll be the weep - ing wil - low drown-ing in my tears,

and   you can go swim - ming   when you are here.   And I'll be the rain - bow

af - ter   the tears are gone,   wrap___ you in my cov - ers   and keep you warm.

That's how strong   my love is,   whoa,_____   that's how strong   my

love___ is.___   That's how strong   my love is,   ba - by,

ba - by,   that's how strong my love is,   I'll be the   o - cean   so deep and wide,

Lemon Tree Will Holt

2. One day beneath the lemon tree, my love and I did lie,
   A girl so sweet that when she smiled, the stars rose in the sky.
   We passed that summer lost in love, beneath the lemon tree,
   The music of her laughter hid my father's words from me.
   Chorus

3. One day she left without a word, she took away the sun.
   And in the dark she left behind, I knew what she had done.
   She left me for another, it's a common tale but true,
   A sadder man, but wiser now, I sing these words to you.
   Chorus

Superstar

Bonnie Bramlett and Leon Russell

Don't you re-mem-ber you told me you love me, ba - by?___ You

said you'd be com - ing back___ this way___ a - gain,___ may - be.___

Ba - by, ba - by, ba - by, ba - by, oh,___ ba - by,___ I

to Coda ⊕ | 1. | 2.

love___ you___ I real - ly do.___ I real - ly do.___

Coda

D.S. al Coda ⊕

⊕

— I real - ly do.___

2. Loneliness is such a sad affair, and I can hardly wait to be with you again.
   What to say, to make you come again?
   Come back to me again, and play your sad guitar.

131

I Want You   Bob Dylan

Alternating thumb style
T i T m T i T
1 & 2 & 3 & 4

Moderately bright

guilt - y un - der - tak - er sighs,___ The lone - some or - gan
drunk - en pol - i - ti - cian leaps___ Up - on the street___ where

grind - er cries,___ The sil - ver sax - o - phones___ say I___ should re - fuse you.
moth - ers weep,___ And the sav - iors who___ are fast___ a - sleep,___ They wait for you.___

___ The cracked bells and washed - out horns___ Blow in - to my
___ And I wait for them to in - ter - rupt___ Me drink - in' from my

face with scorn,_ But it's not that way, I was - n't born___ to lose you.___
bro - ken cup___ And ask me___ to o - pen up___ the gate for you.___

1. The

3. Well, I return to the Queen of Spades
   And talk with my chambermaid.
   Ske knows that I'm not afraid
   To look at her.
   She is good to me
   And there's nothing she doesn't see
   She knows where I'd like to be
   But it doesn't matter.
   Chorus

4. Now your dancing child with his Chinese suit,
   He spoke to me, I took his flute.
   No, I wasn't very cute to him,
   Was I?
   But I did it, though, because he lied
   Because he took you for a ride
   And because time was on his side,
   And because I...
   Chorus

133

Behind Blue Eyes
Pete Townshend

Alternating thumb style
T i T m T i T
1 & 2 & 3 & 4

Moderately

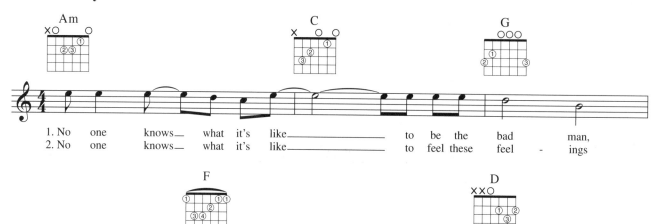

1. No one knows— what it's like_____ to be the bad man,
2. No one knows— what it's like_____ to feel these feel - ings

to be the sad man be - hind blue eyes.—
like I do, and I blame you.—

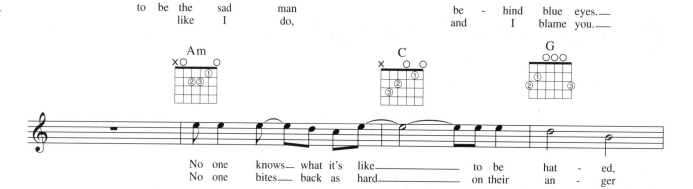

No one knows— what it's like_____ to be hat - ed,
No one bites— back as hard_____ on their an - ger

to be fat - ed to tell - ing on - ly lies. }
none of my pain and woe— can show through.

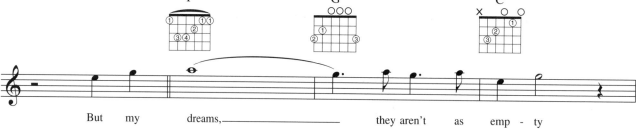

But my dreams,_____ they aren't as emp - ty

Tainted Love   Ed Cobb

Bass-strum style T ↓ T ↑ ↓ ↑
                 1 2 3 & 4 &

With a moving beat

Some - times___ I feel___ I've got to

run a - way,___ I've got to get a - way___ from the pain you

drive___ in - to the heart___ of me.___ The love___ we___ share___

___ seems to go no - where,___ and I've lost___ my light___

___ for___ I toss___ and turn,___ I can't sleep at night.

Leaving on a Jet Plane   John Denver

Alternating thumb style
P i T m T i T
1 & 2 & 3 & 4

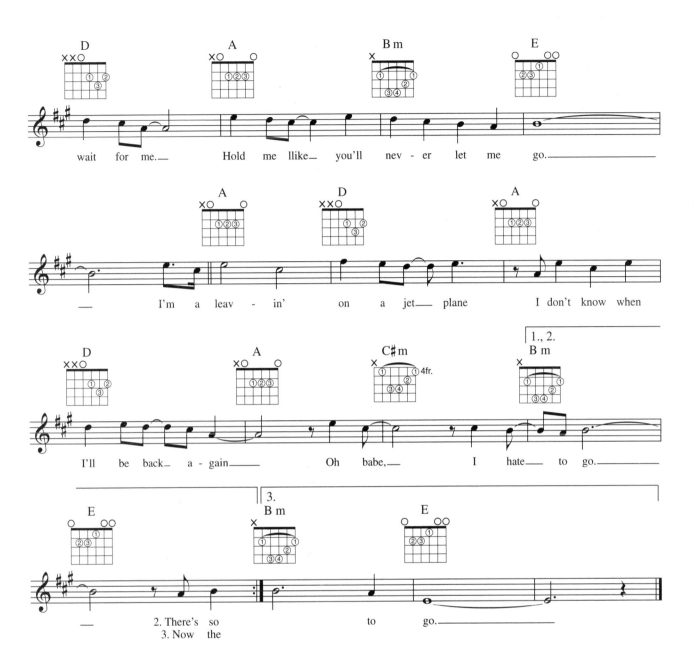

wait for me. **Hold me llike— you'll nev - er let me go.**

— I'm a leav - in' on a jet— plane I don't know when

1., 2.

I'll be back a - gain— Oh babe, I hate— to go.

3.

— to go.—
2. There's so
3. Now the

2. There's so many times, I let you down,
   So many times, I played around,
   But I can tell you, they don't mean a thing.
   Every place I go, I'll think of you,
   Every song I sing, I'll sing for you.
   When I come back, I'll bring your wedding ring.
   Chorus

3. Now the time has come to leave you,
   One more time let me kiss you,
   Then close your eyes, I'll be on my way.
   Dream about the days to come,
   When I won't have to leave alone,
   About the times I won't have to stay.
   Chorus

Puff the Magic Dragon   Peter Yarrow and Leonard Lipton

Alternating thumb style
P i T m T i T
1 & 2 & 3 & 4

Verse

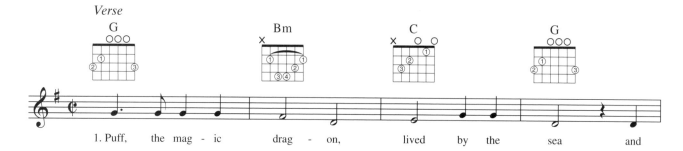

1. Puff,   the mag - ic   drag - on,   lived   by   the   sea   and

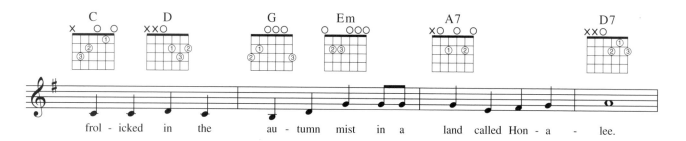

frol - icked   in   the   au - tumn mist   in a   land called Hon - a - lee.

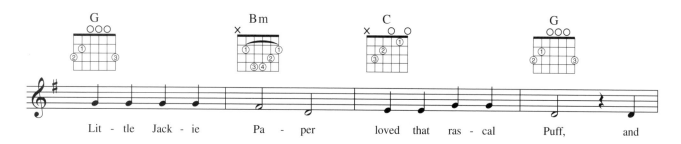

Lit - tle   Jack - ie   Pa - per   loved that   ras - cal   Puff,   and

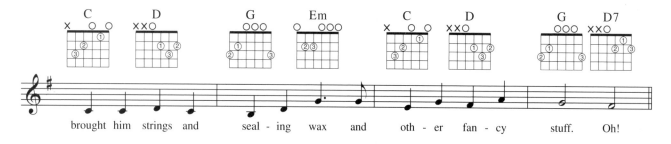

brought him strings   and   seal - ing wax   and   oth - er fan - cy   stuff.   Oh!

Chorus

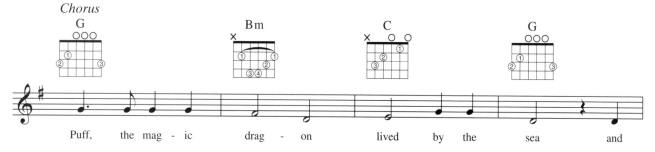

Puff,   the mag - ic   drag - on   lived   by   the   sea   and

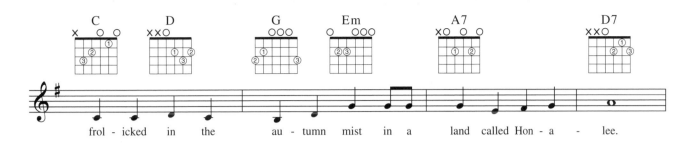

frol - icked in the au - tumn mist in a land called Hon - a - lee.

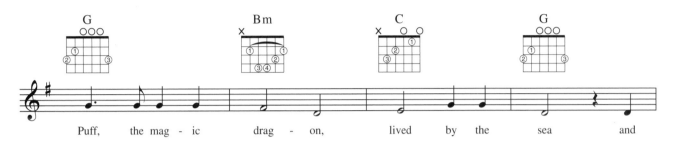

Puff, the mag - ic drag - on, lived by the sea and

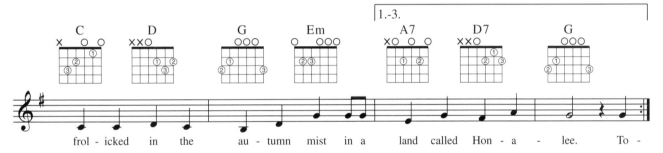

frol - icked in the au - tumn mist in a land called Hon - a - lee. To -

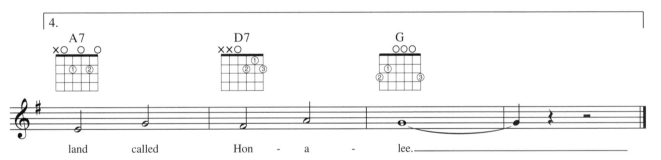

land called Hon - a - lee.

2. Together they would travel on boat with billowed sail.
   Jackie kept a lookout perched on Puff's gigantic tail.
   Noble kings and princes would bow whene'er they came.
   Pirate ships would lower their flags when Puff roared out his name. Oh!
   Chorus

3. A dragon lives forever, but not so little boys.
   Painted wings and giants's rings make way for other toys.
   One grey night it happened, Jackie Paper came no more,
   And Puff that mighty dragon, he ceased his fearless roar.
   Chorus

4. His head was bent in sorrow, green scales fell like rain.
   Puff no longer went to play along the cherry lane.
   Without his lifelong friend, Puff could not be brave,
   So, Puff that mighty dragon sadly slipped into his cave. Oh!
   Chorus

Rainy Day Women #12 & 35   Bob Dylan

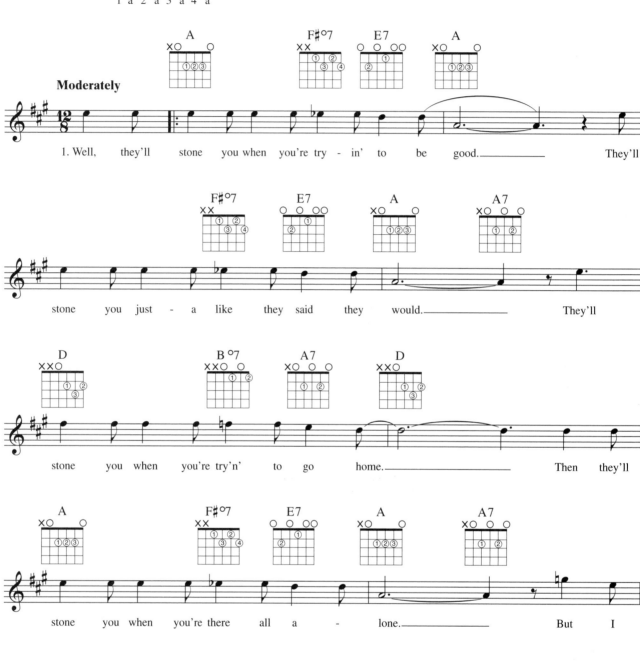

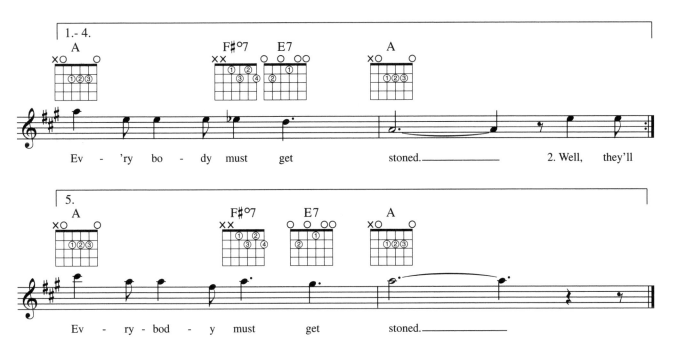

1.- 4.

A   F#°7   E7   A

Ev - 'ry bo - dy must get stoned.————— 2. Well, they'll

5.

A   F#°7   E7   A

Ev - ry - bod - y must get stoned.—————

2. Well, they'll stone you when you're walkin' 'long the street.
   They'll stone you when you're tryin' to keep your seat.
   They'll stone you when you're walkin' on the floor.
   They'll stone you when you're walkin' to the door.
   But I would not feel so all alone,
   Everybody must get stoned.

3. They'll stone you when you're at the breakfast table.
   They'll stone you when you are young and able.
   They'll stone you when you're tryin' to make a buck.
   They'll stone you and then they'll say, "good luck."
   Tell ya what, I would not feel so all alone,
   Everybody must get stoned.

4. Well, they'll stone you and say that it's the end.
   Then they'll stone you and then they'll come back again.
   They'll stone you when you're riding in your car.
   They'll stone you when you're playing your guitar.
   Yes, but I would not feel so all alone.
   Everybody must get stoned.

5. Well, they'll stone you when you walk all alone.
   They'll stone you when you are walking home.
   They'll stone you and then say you are brave.
   They'll stone you when you are set down in your grave.
   But I would not feel so all alone,
   Everybody must get stoned.

Teach Your Children   Graham Nash

Alternating thumb style
P i T m T i T
1 & 2 & 3 & 4

Moderately

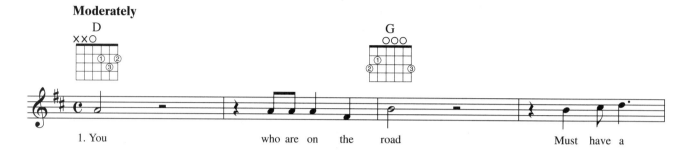

1. You   who are on the   road   Must have a

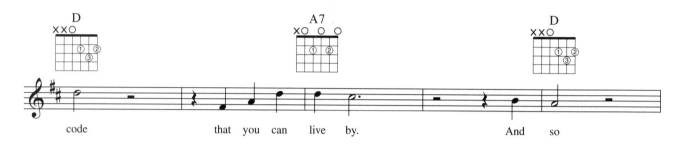

code   that you can live by.   And so

be - come your - self   Be - cause the   past   is just a

Chorus

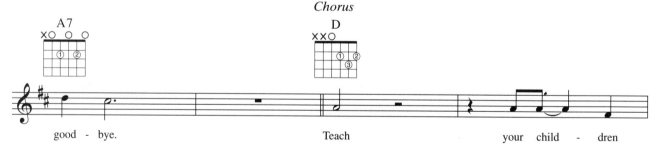

good - bye.   Teach   your child - dren

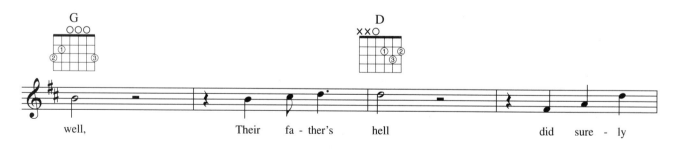

well,   Their fa - ther's hell   did sure - ly

go by.   And   feed   them   on   your dreams,

The   one they picks,   the   one you'll know   by.

Don't you   ev - er   ask   them   why,   If   they told   you,   you   will

cry,   so just   look   at   them   and   sigh_____

and   know   they   love_____ you.   2. And

2. And you, of tender years,
   Can't know the fears
   That your elders grew by.
   And so please help them with your youth,
   They seek the truth before they can die.

   Chorus
   Teach your parents well,
   Their children's hell will slowly go by.
   And feed them on your dreams,
   The one they picks, the one you'll know by.

   Don't you ever ask them why, if they told you, you would cry,
   So just look at them and sigh and know they love you.

Wild World   Cat Stevens

Strumming swing style ↓ ↓ ↓ ↓↑ ↓↑ ↓ ↓ ↓↑
1 & 2 &a 3 a & 4 &a

Slowly

1. Now that I've lost ev-'ry-thing to you___ you say you wan-na start some-thing new___

___ and it's break-ing my heart_ you're leav - ing. Ba - by. I'm griev - in'!

But if you want to leave take good care, hope you have a lot of nice things to wear___

___ but then a lot of nice things turn bad out there.___

Oh ba - by, ba - by it's a wild world.

It's hard to get by_ just up-on a smile. Oh, ba - by, ba - by it's a

Coda

D.S. al Coda

child, girl.

2. You know I've seen a lot of what the world can do,
   And it's breaking my heart in two,
   Because I never want to see you sad, girl.
   Don't be bad girl.
   But if you want to leave take good care,
   Hope you make a lot of nice friends out there
   But just remember there's a lot of bad and beware.

Take Me Home, Country Roads

John Denver, Bill Danoff
and Taffy Nivert

Alternating thumb style
P i T m T i T
1 & 2 & 3 & 4

Coda

roads._____ Coun - try roads,_____ take__ me home_____ __ to the place_____ I be - long;_____ __ West Vir - gin - ia,_____ moun - tain mam - ma,_____ __ Take__ me home,_____ Coun - try roads,_____ __ take__ me home,_____ Coun - try roads,_____ __ Take__ me home,_____ Coun - try roads._____

2. All my memories gather 'round her,
Miner's lady, stranger to blue water.
Dark and dusty, painted on the sky,
Misty taste of moonshine, teardrop in my eye.

Hard Headed Woman

Cat Stevens

Strumming style ↓ ↓ ↓ ↓↑ ↓↑ ↓ ↓ ↓↑

1 & 2 &a 3a & 4 &a

I know the rest of my life___ will be blessed, yes, yes, yes.___

___ I know a lot of fan - cy danc - ers,

Peo - ple who can glide you___ on a floor,___

They move so slow___ but have no an - swers___

when you ask___ why'd you come here for? *spoken* Why?
(I don't know)

I know   man - y   fine   feath - ered   friends___ but their
They know   man - y   sure - fired___   ways___   to find

friend - li-ness de - pends_____ on how you do.___
out the one who pays_____ and how you do.___

I'm look-ing for a hard head-ed wom - an.___

one who will make__ me feel so good._____

And if I find my hard head-ed wom - an___

D.S. al Coda

I know my life will be as___ it should, yes, yes, yes.___

Coda

Fly Me to the Moon (In Other Words)

Bart Howard

Tonight I'll Be Staying Here with You

Bob Dylan

Strumming style ↓ ↓ ↓ ↑ ↓ ↑
                  1 2 3 & 4 &

Moderately slow, with a beat

Throw my tick-et out the win-dow,

Throw my suit-case out there, too.— Throw my

trou-bles out the door, I don't need them an-y more, 'cause to-

night I'll be stay-ing here with you.

Mrs. Robinson Paul Simon

Alternating thumb style
P i T m T i T
1 & 2 & 3 & 4

Moderately

Chorus

And here's to you,— Mrs.— Rob - in - son,— Je - sus loves you more—

— than you— will know,— Wo, wo, wo.— God bless you

please, Mrs.— Rob - in - son,— Heav - en holds— a place—

— for those— who pray,— Hey, hey, hey.—

Verse

— Hey, hey, hey.— 1. We'd

like to know a lit - tle bit— a - bout— you for our files.—

3. Sitting on a sofa on a Sunday afternoon.
   Going to the candidates debate.
   Laugh about it, shout about it,
   When you've got to choose,
   Ev'ry way you look at it, you lose.

   Chorus:
   Where have you gone, Joe DiMaggio?
   A nation turns its lonely eyes to you. Woo, woo, woo.
   What's that you say, Mrs. Robinson?
   Joltin' Joe has left and gone away.
   Hey, hey, hey. Hey, hey, hey.

The Complete Guitar Player Songbook

Book 3

by Russ Shipton

166 Killing Me Softly
168 Leader of the Band
170 Bridge Over Troubled Water
173 Perfect World
176 Goodbye Yellow Brick Road
178 Make You Feel My Love
180 Simple Twist of Fate
182 Sorry Seems to Be the Hardest Word
184 What a Wonderful World +
186 You Are So Beautiful
188 Helplessly Hoping
191 I Feel the Earth Move
194 Annie's Song
196 The Best of My Love
198 What a Difference a Day Makes

200 Baby Hold On
203 Kodachrome™
206 America
210 Let's Groove
213 Rocket Man +
216 Still Crazy after All These Years
219 I Remember You
220 Send in the Clowns
222 April Come She Will
224 Endless Love +
226 Lovin' You
228 Jesus Is Just Alright
231 Fifty Ways to Leave Your Lover
234 Lay, Lady, Lay +
238 Rainy Days and Mondays

Amsco Publications
A Part of **The Music Sales Group**
New York/London/Paris/Sydney/Copenhagen/Berlin/Tokyo/Madrid

Killing Me Softly with His Song

Norman Gimbel
and Charles Fox

Arpeggio T i m T i m T i
1 & 2 & 3 & 4 &

Moderately

Verse

1. I heard— he sang— a good— song I heard he had— — a style. And so— I came— to see— him to lis - ten for a - while.——— And there— he was— — this young— boy a stran - ger to—— my eyes.———

Chorus

Strum - ming my pain— with his fin - gers,——— Sing - ing my life— with his words.—

Kill - ing me soft - ly with his____ song. Kill - ing me soft -

ly____ with his____ song. Tell - ing my whole___ life_____ with his___

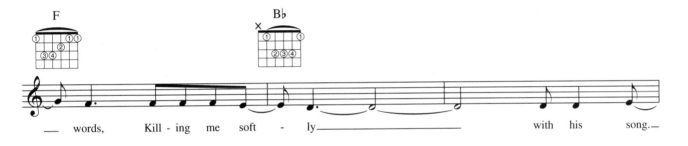

___ words, Kill - ing me soft - ly_____ with his song.___

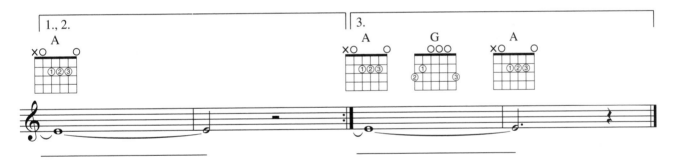

2. I felt all flushed with fever
   Embarrassed by the crowd.
   I felt he found my letters
   And read each one out loud.
   I prayed that he would finish
   But he just kept right on.
   Chorus

3. He sang as if he knew me
   In all my dark despair.
   And then he looked right through me
   As if I wasn't there.
   And he just kept on singing
   Singing clear and strong.
   Chorus

Leader of the Band   Dan Fogelberg

Alternating thumb style P T i T m T
1 2 & 3 & 4

Moderately

1. An on - ly child, a - lone and wild;— A cab - 'net mak - er's

son. His hands were meant for dif - f'rent work and his

heart was known to none.— He left his home and

went his lone— and sol - i - tar - y way. And he gave to me a

gift I know I nev - er can re - pay.

The lead - er of the band is tired, his eyes are grow - ing

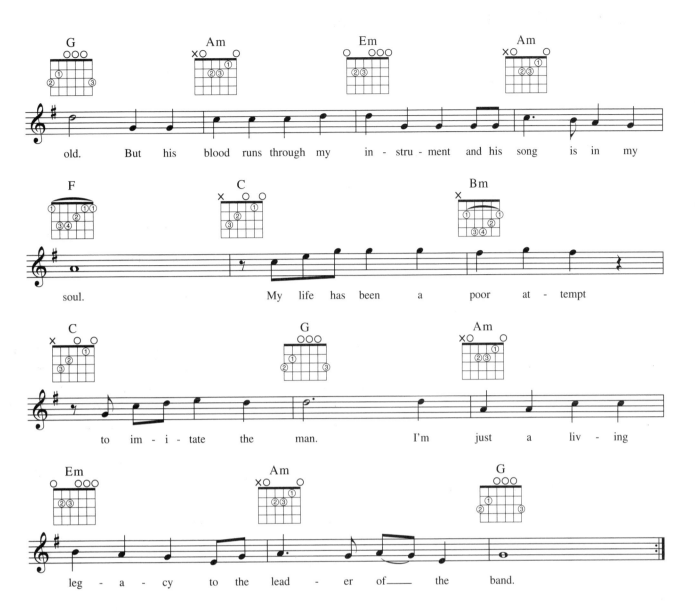

2. A quiet man of music,
   Denied a simpler fate.
   He tried to be a soldier once
   But his music wouldn't wait.
   He earned his love through discipline,
   A thundering velvet hand.
   His gentle means of sculpting souls
   Took me years to understand.

3. My brother's lives were different
   For they heard another call.
   One went to Chicago and the other to St. Paul.
   And I'm in Colorado
   When I'm not in some hotel,
   Living out this life I've chose
   And come to know so well.

4. I thank you for the music
   And your stories of the road.
   I thank you for the freedom
   When it came my time to go.
   I thank you for the kindness
   And the times when you got tough.
   And papa I don't think I said
   "I love you" near enough.

Bridge Over Troubled Water   Paul Simon

Bass-strum style T ↓ ↑ T ↑ ↓ ↑
1 2 & 3 & 4 &

Moderately, not too fast

down.   Like   a   Bridge   o - ver   trou - bled   wa - ter

I will lay   me   down.   When you're   Trou-bled   wa-ter

I   will   lay   me   down.

Sail on   sil - ver girl,   Sail   on   by,

Your   time   has   come   to   shine.   All   your   dreams   are   on   their   way.

See   how   they   shine.   Oh,   if   you

2. When you're down and out, when you're on the street,
   when evening falls so hard, I'll comfort you.
   I'll take your part, oh, when darkness comes and pain is all around,

Perfect World   Alex Call

Bass-strum style T ↓ ↑ T ↑ ↓ ↑
1 2 & 3 & 4 &

Moderate rock

1. Ev - 'ry-bod - y's look - in' for a per - fect world,___

where you could have ev - 'ry - thing your heart de - sires.

The per - fect boy will meet the per - fect girl.___

and their per - fect love will set the world on fire.

What you gon - na do when one and one___ makes three

2. Everybody's got secrets, now you know that it's true.
They talk about me and they'll talk about you.
Something happens to the pledges of trust.
Down through the years they begin to rust.
Now here we are amid the tears and the laughter,
Still waiting for our happily ever after.
We'll keep on dreamin' as long as we can,
Try to remember and you'll understand.

Goodbye Yellow Brick Road

Elton John & Bernie Taupin

Arpeggio T i m T i m T i
1 & 2 & 3 & 4 &

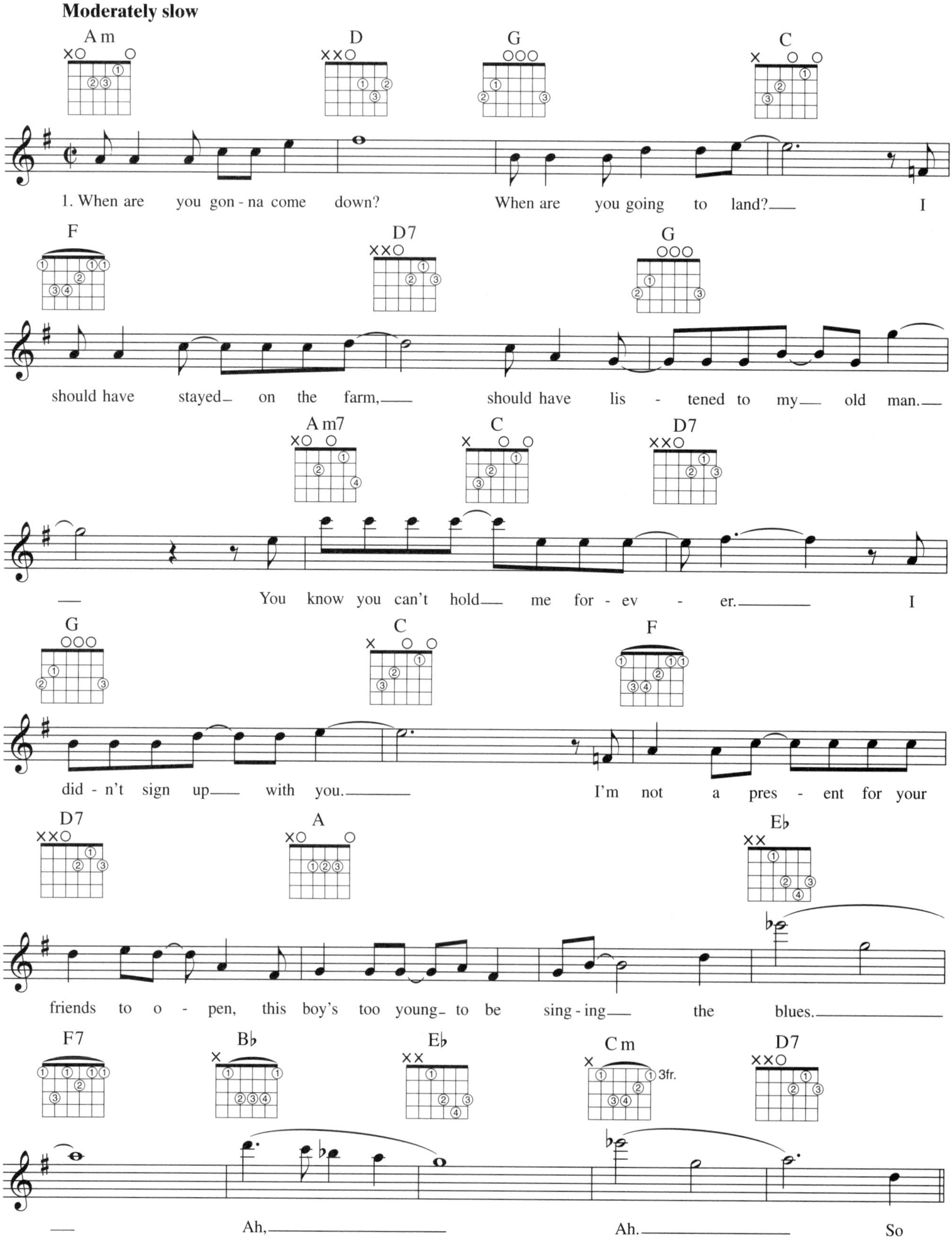

Moderately slow
Am D G C
1. When are you gon - na come down? When are you going to land? I
F D7 G
should have stayed on the farm, should have lis - tened to my old man.
Am7 C D7
You know you can't hold me for - ev - er. I
G C F
did - n't sign up with you. I'm not a pres - ent for your
D7 A E♭
friends to o - pen, this boy's too young to be sing - ing the blues.
F7 B♭ E♭ Cm D7
Ah, Ah. So
3fr.

good-bye— yel-low brick road,_____ Where the dogs of so-ci-et-y howl.— You

can't plant me in your pent-house,_____ I'm go-ing back— to my plough.

Back to the howl-ing old owl___ in the woods— hunt-ing the horn-y back

toad. Oh I've fi – n'lly de-cid-ed my fu-ture lies be-

yond the yel-low brick road._____ Ah,—

— Ah,_____ Ah. Ah.

2. What do you think you'll do then?
I bet that'll shoot down your plane.
It'll take you a couple of vodka and tonics
To set you our feet again.

Maybe you'll get a replacement,
There's plenty like me to be found.
Mongrels who ain't got a penny
Sniffing for tidbits like you on the ground.

Make You Feel My Love   Bob Dylan

Arpeggio T i m i m i T i
1 & 2 & 3 & 4 &

Moderately slow

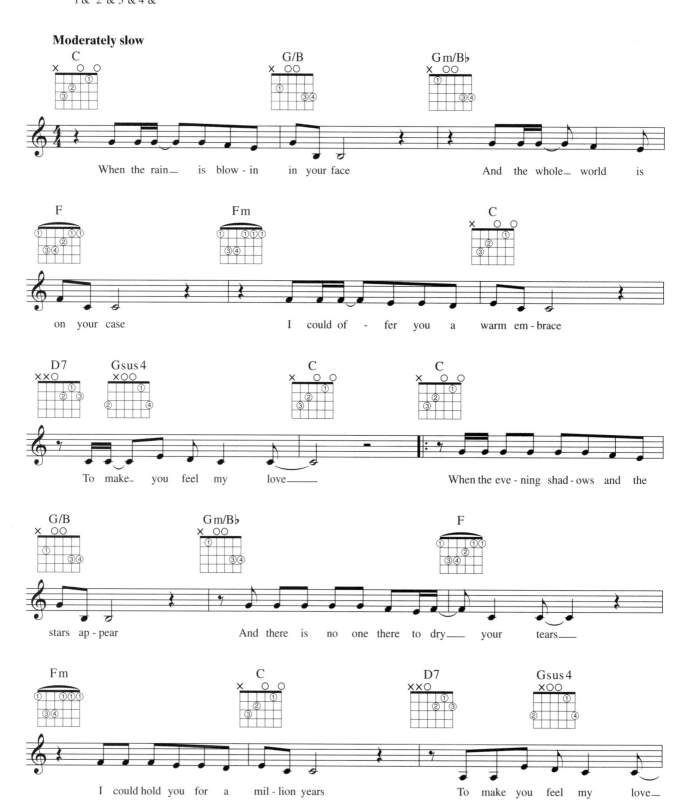

When the rain— is blow - in in your face   And the whole— world is

on your case   I could of - fer you a warm em - brace

To make— you feel my love_____   When the eve - ning shad - ows and the

stars ap - pear   And there is no one there to dry___ your tears___

I could hold you for a mil - lion years   To make you feel my love—

Simple Twist of Fate   Bob Dylan

Strumming style ↓ ↑ ↓ ↑ ↓ ↑ ↓ ↑
           1 & 2 & 3 & 4 &

Moderately

1. They sat to-geth-er in the park, as the eve-ning sky___ grew dark.

She looked at him and he felt a spark tin-gle to___ his bones.___

___ 'Twas then he felt a - lone___ and wished___

___ that he'd gone straight,___ And watched out___ for a

sim-ple twist of fate.___ They walked a - long by the old___

___ ca - nal,___ a lit-tle con-fused, I re-mem-ber well,

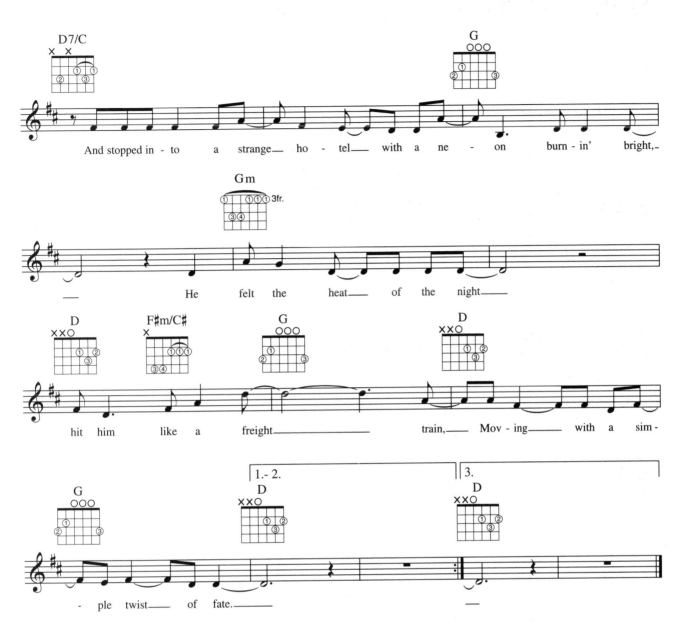

2. A saxophone someplace far off played
   As she was walkin' by the arcade.
   As the light bust through a beat-up shade where he was wakin' up,
   She dropped a coin into the cup of a blind man at the gate
   And forgot about a simple twist of fade.

   He woke up, the room was bare
   He didn't see her anywhere.
   He told himself he didn't care, pushed the window open wide,
   Felt an emptiness inside to which he just could not relate
   Brought on by a simple twist of fate.

3. He hears the ticking of the clocks
   And walks along with a parrot that talks,
   Hunts her down by the waterfront docks where the sailers all come in.
   Maybe she'll pick him out again, how long must he wait
   Once more for a simple twist of fate.

   People tell me it's a sin
   To know and feel too much within.
   I still believe she was my twin, but I lost the ring.
   She was born in spring, but I was born too late
   Blame it on a simple twist of fate.

Sorry Seems to Be the Hardest Word

Elton John &
Bernie Taupin

Arpeggio T i m r T i m r
1 & 2 & 3 & 4 &

Slow Ballad

What have I got to do to make you love me? What have I got to do to make you care?

What do I do when light-ning strikes me and I wake to find that you're not there?

What do I do to make you want me? What have I got to do—— to be heard?

What do I say when it's all o-ver? Sor-ry seems to be the hard-est

What a Wonderful World

George David Weiss and Bob Thiele

Bass-strum style

The col - ors of the rain - bow, so pret - ty in the sky are

al - so on the fac - es of peo - ple go - in' by. I see friends shak - in' hands, say - in'

D.S. al Coda

"How do you do?" They're real - ly say - in' "I love you." 3. I hear

Coda

world. Yes, I think to my - self

what a won - der - ful world.

3. I hear babies cry, I watch them grow;
   They'll learn much more than I'll never know
   And I think to myself, what a wonderful world
   Yes I think to myself, what a wonderful world.

You Are So Beautiful

Billy Preston and Bruce Fisher

Arpeggio T i m r T i m r
1 & 2 & 3 & 4 &

Moderately

You are so beau-ti - ful___ to___ me.

You are so beau-ti - ful___ to___

me.   Can't you see___   you're ev - 'ry - thing   that I

hope   for   and what's   more,   you're ev - 'ry - thing   I

need.___   You   are   so   beau - ti - ful   ba - by   to

Helplessly Hoping Stephen Stills

Alternating thumb style
P T i T m T
1 2 & 3 & 4

Moderately

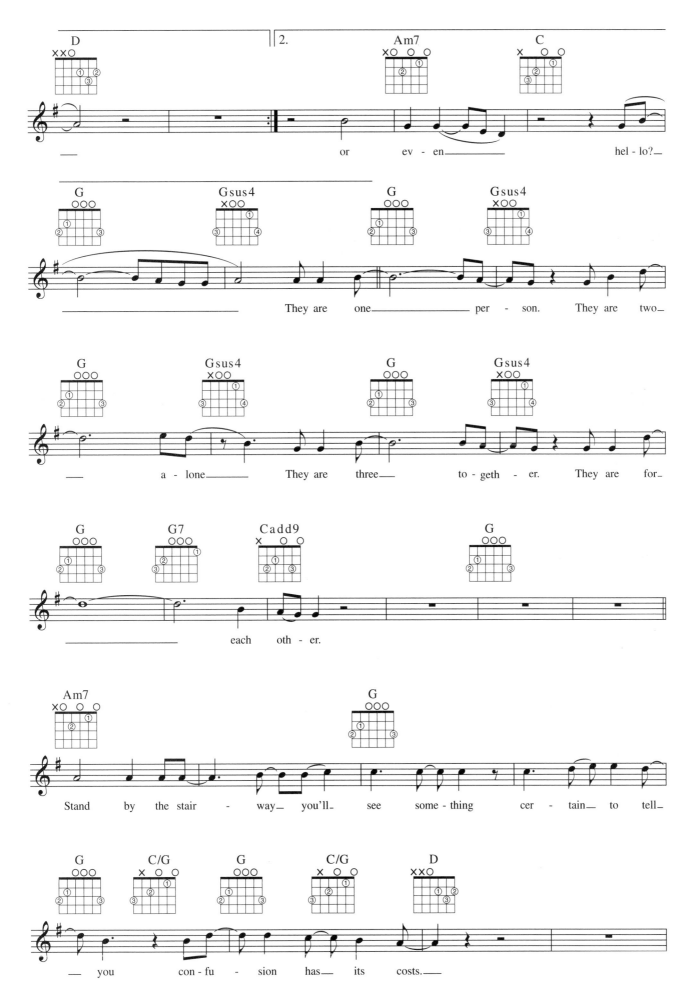

I Feel the Earth Move
Carole King

Strumming style/half bar stress

↓ ↓ ↑   ↑ ↓

1 2 &(3) & 4

Moderately

I feel the earth move un-der my feet;__ I feel the

sky__ tum-bl-in' down__ I feel my heart start to trem-bl-in'__

__ when-ev-er__ you're a-round.__ Ooh,__ ba-

-by,__ when I see__ your face,__ mel-low as the month of__ May,__

__ Oh,__ dar-lin',__ I can't stand__ it when you look

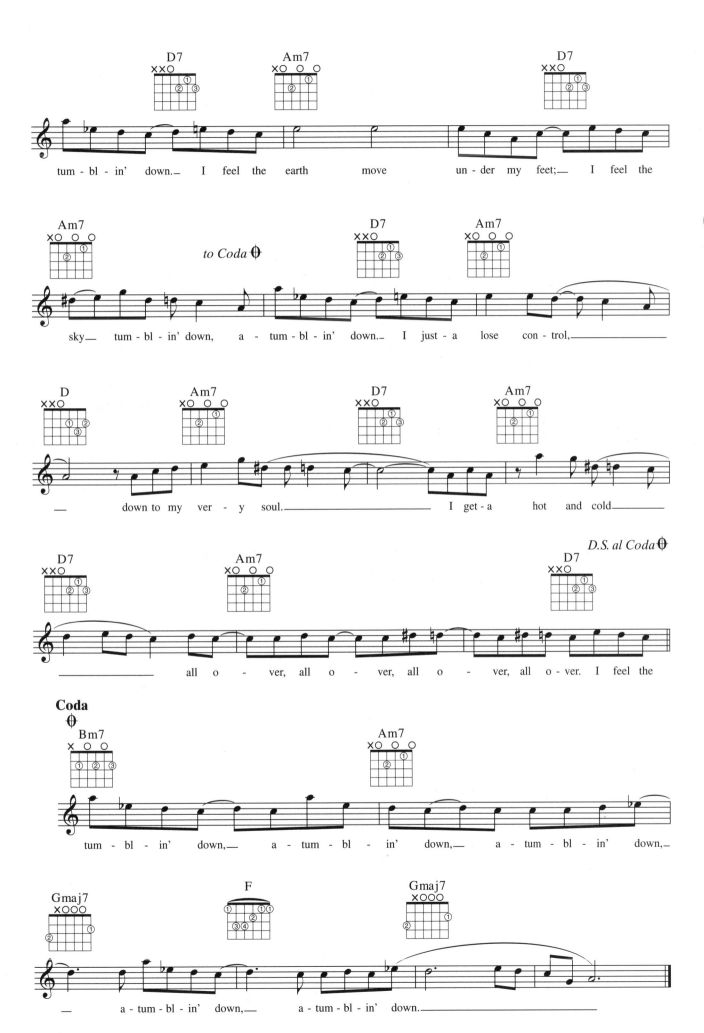

Annie's Song   John Denver

Strumming style T ↓ ↑ ↓
1 2 & 3

Moderately

Best of My Love

John David Souther, Don Henley and Glenn Frey

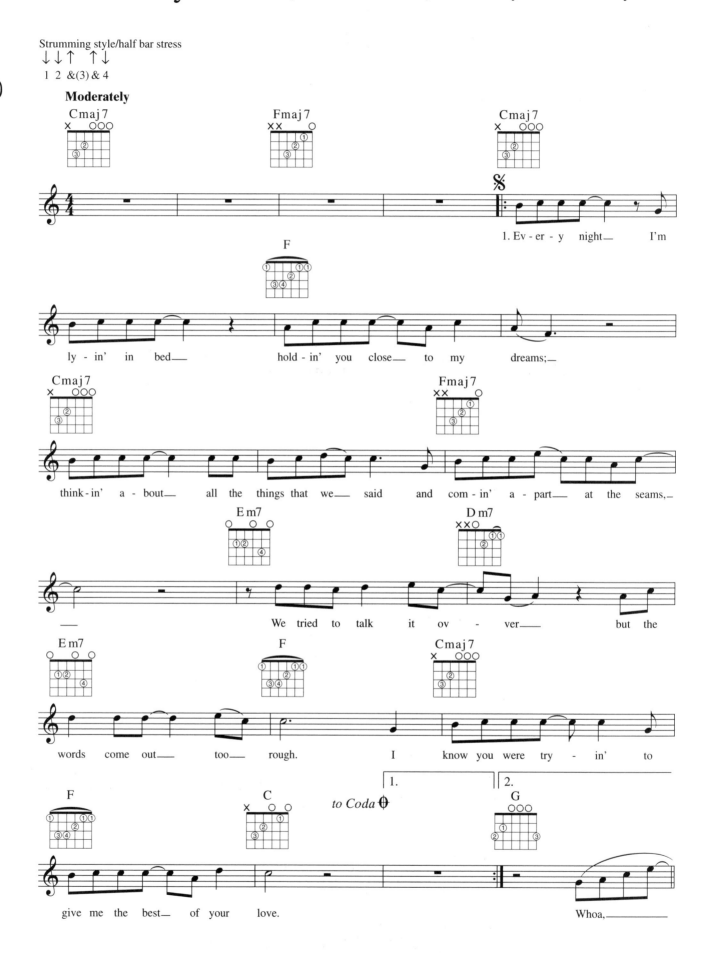

Strumming style/half bar stress

2. Beautiful faces and loud empty places, look at the way we live;
   Wasting our time on cheap talk and wine, left us so little to give.
   That same old crowd was like a cold dark cloud that we could never rise above.
   But here in my heart I give you the best of my love.

3. But every morning I wake up and worry what's gonna happen today.
   You see it your way and I see it mine but we both see it slipping away.
   You know we always had each other, baby, I guess that wasn't enough;
   Oh, oh, but here in my heart I give you the best of my love.

What a Difference a Day Makes

Maria Grever
and Stanley Adams

Baby Hold On

Eddie Money and James Douglas Lyon

Strumming style/half bar stress

↓ ↓ ↑   ↑ ↓
1 2 & (3) & 4

Moderately fast

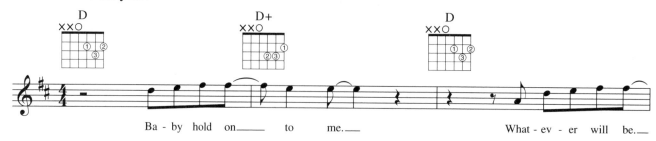

Ba - by hold on____ to me.____ What - ev - er will be.____

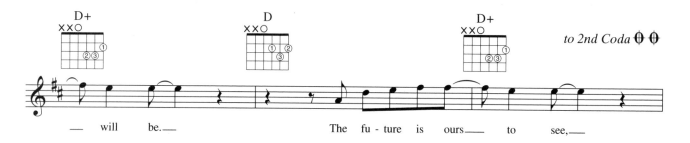

— will be.____ The fu - ture is ours____ to see,____

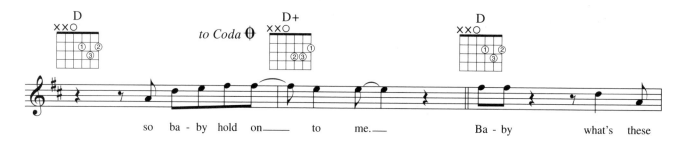

so ba - by hold on____ to me.____ Ba - by what's these

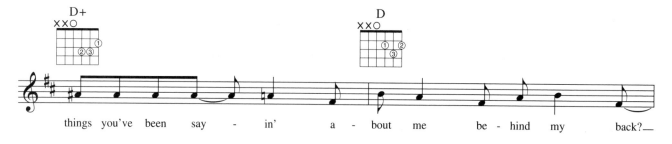

things you've been say - in' a - bout me be - hind my back?____

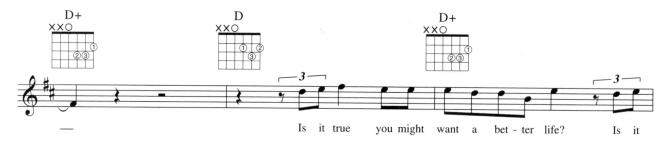

— Is it true you might want a bet - ter life? Is it

So baby hold on to me.
Whatever will be, will be (I say).
The future is ours to see.
When you hold on to me.

You know the future's lookin' brighter
Every mornin' when I get up.
Don't be thinkin' 'bout what's not enough, now baby,
Just be thinkin' 'bout what we got.
Think of all my love, now.
I'm gonna give you all I got.

Kodachrome™ Paul Simon

Bass-strum style T ↓ ↑ T ↑ ↓ ↑
1 2 & 3 & 4 &

Moderately with a beat

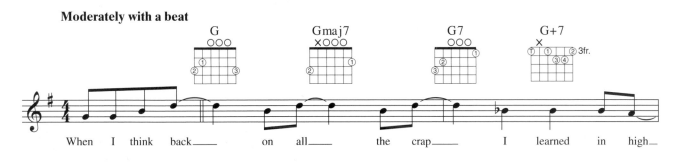

When I think back___ on all___ the crap___ I learned in high___

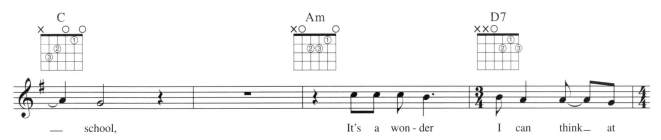

___ school, It's a won-der I can think___ at

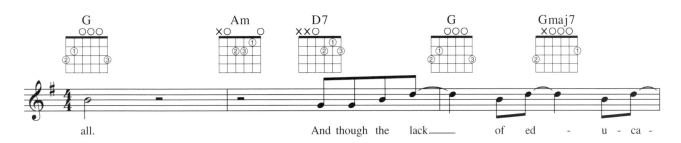

all. And though the lack___ of ed - u - ca-

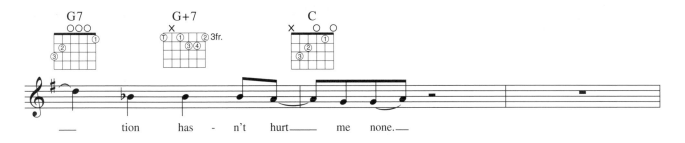

___ tion has - n't hurt___ me none.___

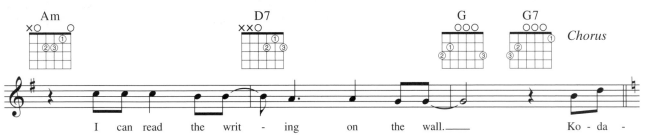

I can read the writ - ing on the wall.___ Ko - da -

* "KODACHROME" is a registered trademark for color film.

Book 2 Pages 12-14

204

America   Paul Simon

Strumming style ↓ ↓ ↑ ↓
        1 2 & 3

Bright waltz tempo

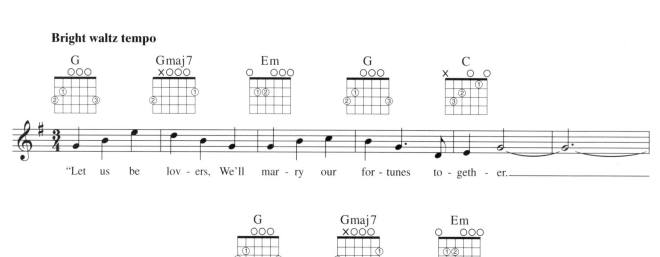

"Let us be lov - ers, We'll mar - ry our for - tunes to - geth - er._____

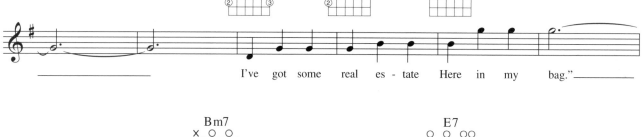

_____ I've got some real es - tate Here in my bag."_____

_____ So we bought a pack of cig - a rettes,_____ And

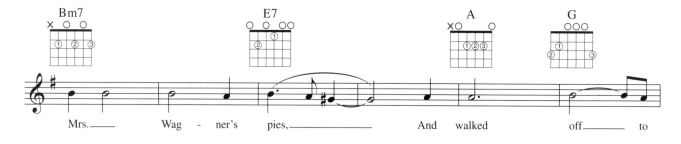

Mrs._____ Wag - ner's pies,_____ And walked off_____ to

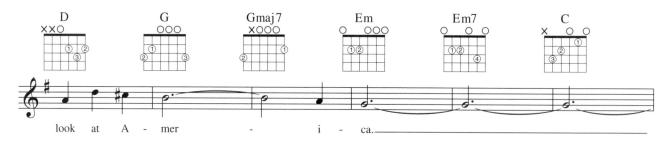

look at A - mer - i - ca._____

206

I said, "Be care - ful, His bow - tie is

real - ly a cam - 'ra."

"Toss me a cig - a - rette, I think there's

one in my rain - coat." "We smoked the

last one An hour a - go." So I

looked at the scen - er - y, She read her mag - a - zine;

— And the moon rose o - ver an o - pen

Let's Groove

Wayne Vaughn and Maurice White

| Am7 | Bm7 | Em |

time, come and see you and me, make a lit - tle sign.

| Cm7 | Dm7 | Gm7 | Bm7♭5 |

I'll be there af - ter a - while if you want my love._____ We can

| B7 | Em | B7 | Em |

boog - ie on down down, boog-ie on down,

| B7 | Em | B7 | Em7 |

down, boog-ie on down, down, boog-ie on down, on

| B7 | Em7 | B7 | Em9 |

down, boog - ie on down.

2. Let this groove, light up your fuse, alright
Let this groove, set in your shoes
Stand up, alright
Let me tell you what you can do
With my love, alright
Gotta let you know girl you're looking good
you're out of sight, you're alright
Tell the DJ to play your favorite tune
Then you know it's okay
What you found is happiness, now

212

Rocket Man
(I Think It's Gonna Be a Long, Long Time)

Elton John & Bernie Taupin

Bass-strum style T ↓ ↑ ↓ ↑ ↓ ↑
1 2 & 3 & 4 &

Moderately slow, with a beat

She packed— my bags— last night pre - flight,—

Ze - ro hour—— nine a. m.——

And I'm gon - na be high—— as a kite by

then.

I miss— the earth— so much,——

miss my wife,—— it's lone - ly out— in space.—

Still Crazy after All These Years

Paul Simon

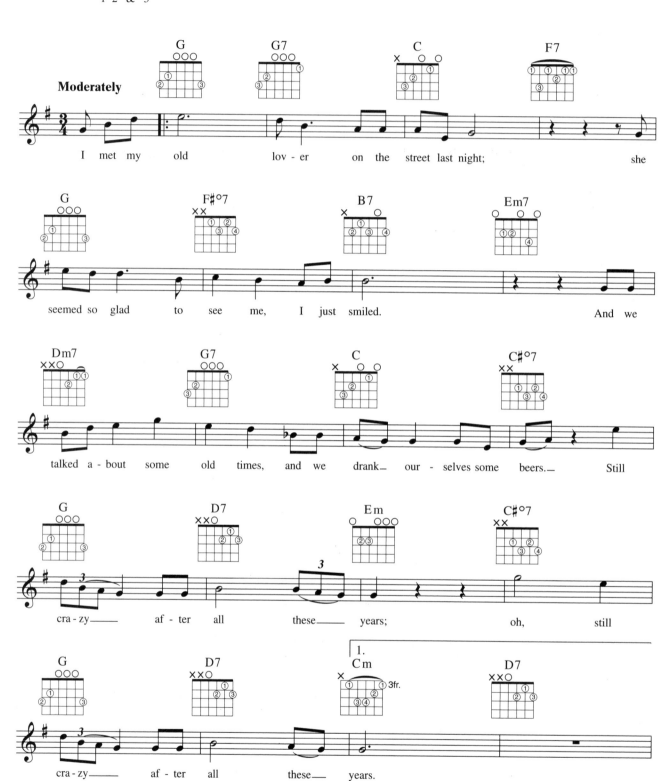

2. I'm not the years.

Four in the morn - ing; crapped out, yawn - ing;

long - ing my life a - way.

I'll nev - er wor - ry; why should I?

It's all gon - na fade.

Now I

sit by my win - dow and I watch my cars; I

217

2. I'm not the kind of man
   Who tends to socialize,
   I seem to lean on
   Old familiar ways.
   And I ain't no fool for love songs
   That whisper in my ears.
   Still crazy after all these years,
   Oh, still crazy after all these years.

I Remember You Johnny Mercer and Victor Schertzinger

Bass-strum style T ↓ ↑ T ↑ ↓ ↑
1 2 & 3 & 4 &

Moderately

2. I remember you,
You're the one who said
"I love you, too," I do.
Didn't you know?

Send in the Clowns   Stephen Sondheim

April Come She Will   Paul Simon

Bass-strum style with hammer

T ↓ ↑ T ↓ ↑
1 2 & 3 & 4 &
　　　H

Moderately

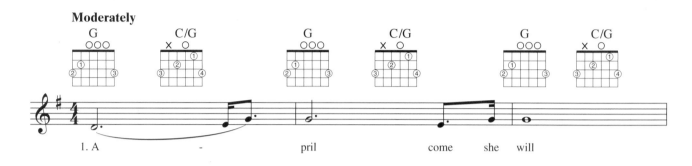

1. A - pril   come   she   will

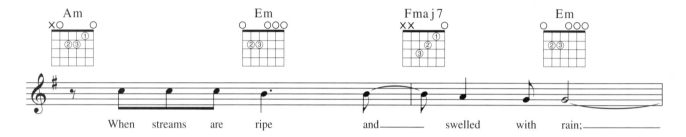

When   streams   are   ripe   and_____   swelled   with   rain;_____

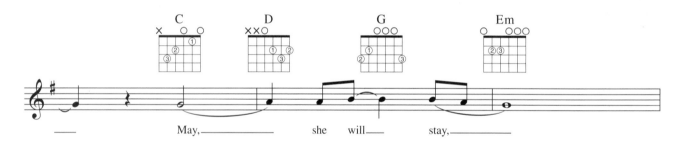

____   May,_____   she   will____   stay,_____

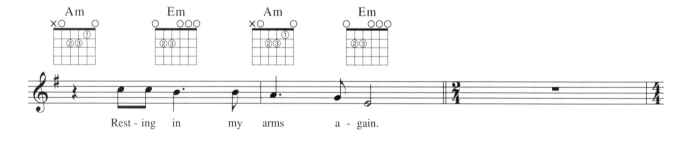

Rest - ing   in   my   arms   a - gain.

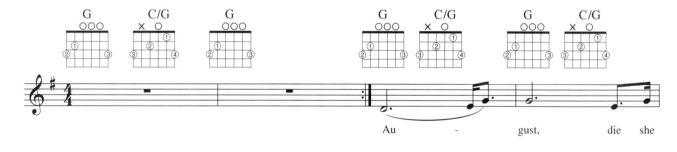

Au -   gust,   die   she

222

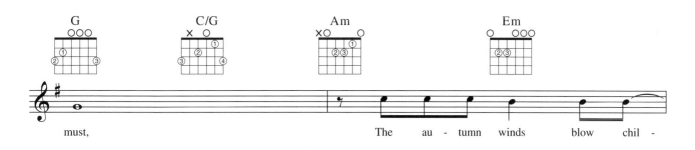

must,   The au - tumn winds blow chil -

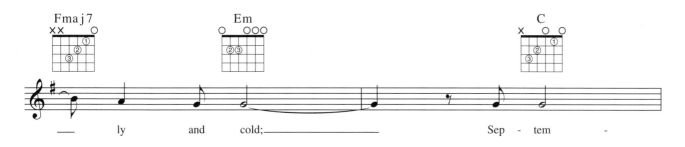

— ly   and   cold;_____   Sep - tem -

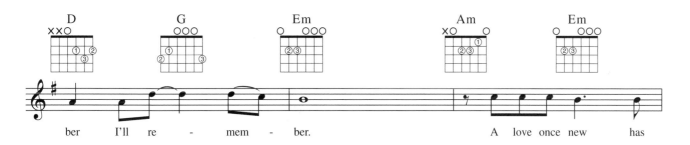

ber I'll re - mem - ber.   A love once new   has

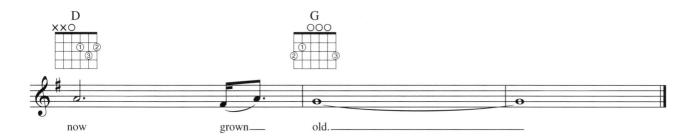

now   grown___ old._____

2. June she'll change her tune,
   In restless walks she'll prowl the night;
   July she will fly.
   And give no warning to her flight.

Endless Love Lionel Richie

Arpeggio T i m r T i m r
1 & 2 & 3 & 4 &

Slow ballad

No one else will— do and your eyes,— they tell me how much you care.———— Oh,———— yes you will al - ways be my end - less

1. love.————

2. love.————

2. Two hearts, Two hearts that beat as one.
Our lives have just begun.
Forever I'll hold you close in my arms.
I can't resist your charm.
And love, I'll be a fool for you. I'm sure.
You know I don't mind 'cause you
You mean the world to me.
Oh yes I've found you
My endless love.

Lovin' You

Minnie Riperton and Richard Rudolph

Jesus Is Just Alright   Arthur Reynolds

Fifty Ways to Leave Your Lover

Paul Simon

Arpeggio T i m r T i m r
1 & 2 & 3 & 4 &

Moderately

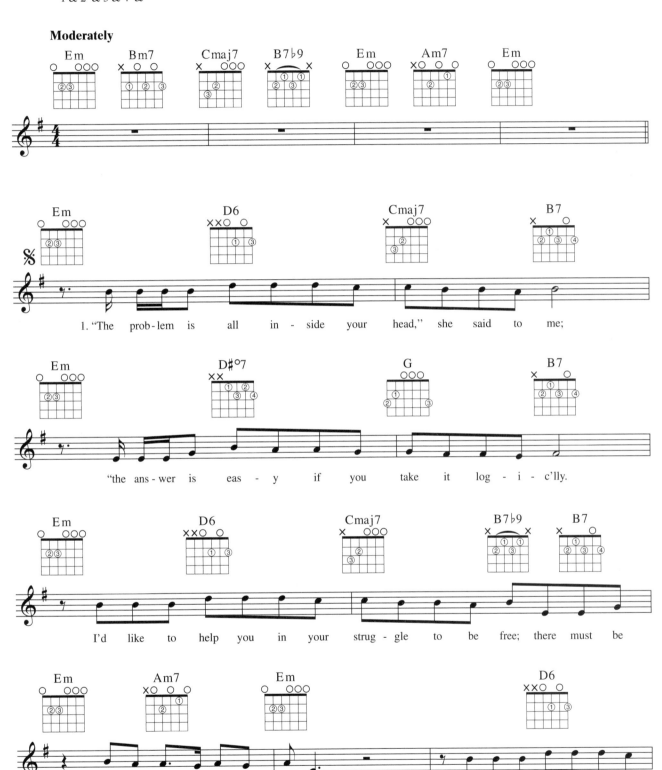

1. "The prob-lem is all in-side your head," she said to me;

"the ans-wer is eas - y if you take it log - i - c'lly.

I'd like to help you in your strug - gle to be free; there must be

fif - ty ways to leave your lov - er." She said, "It's real - ly not my

hab - it to in - trude; I hope my mean - ing won't be lost or mis - con - strued. But

I'll re - peat my - self at the risk of be - ing crude; there must be

fif - ty ways to leave your lo - ver. Fif - ty ways to leave your

Bass-strum style

lov - er." Just slip out the back, Jack; make a new

plan, Stan; you don't need to be coy, Roy,

{ 1. just get your - self free, }
{ 2. just lis - ten to me. } Hop on the bus, Gus;

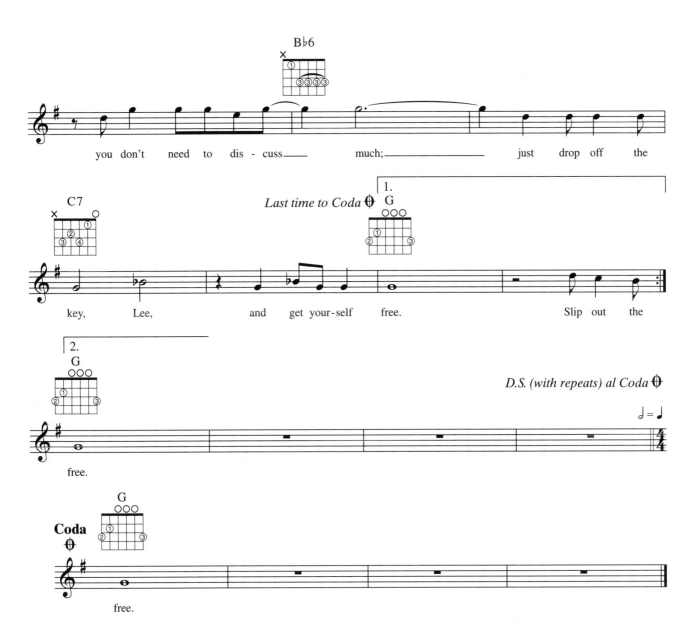

you don't need to dis - cuss____ much;_____ just drop off the

Last time to Coda

key, Lee, and get your-self free. Slip out the

D.S. (with repeats) al Coda

free.

Coda

free.

2. She said, "It grieves me so to see you in such pain.
   I wish there was something I could do to make you smile again."
   I said, "I appreciate that and would you please explain
   About the fifty ways?"

   She said, "Why don't we both just sleep on it tonight,
   And I believe in the morning you'll begin to see the light."
   And then she kissed me and I realized she probably was right.
   There must be fifty ways to leave your lover.
   Fifty ways to leave your lover.

Lay, Lady, Lay Bob Dylan

Rainy Days and Mondays

Paul Williams and Roger Nichols

Alternating thumb style P Ti Tm T P Ti Tm T
1 &a 2a & 3 &a 4a &

Moderately

1. Talk - in' to my - self and feel - in' old,

some - times I'd like to quit noth - ing ev - er seems to fit.

Hang - in' a - round noth - ing to do but frown;

Rain - y days and Mon - days al - ways get me down.

2. What I've got they used to call the blues.
   Nothin' is really wrong,
   Feelin' like I don't belong.
   Walkin' around,
   Some kind of lonely clown.
   Rainy days and Mondays always get me down.

3. What I feel has come and gone before.
   No need to talk it out,
   We know what it's all about.
   Hangin' around,
   Nothing to do but frown.
   Rainy days and Mondays always get me down.